The Winds of God

The Canadian Church
Faces the 1980s

by Rodney M. Booth

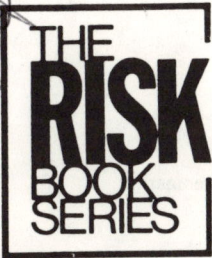

THE RISK BOOK SERIES

Published by
The World Council of Churches
Geneva
in co-operation with
Wood Lake Books, Inc.
Winfield BC Canada

Canadian Cataloguing in Publication Data

Booth, Rodney M.
    The Winds of God
    (Risk book series)
    Bibliography: p.
    ISBN 0-919599-05-2

    1. Canada - Church history. 2. Church and
the world. 3. Sociology, Christian - Canada.
1. World Council of Churches. II. Title.
III. Series
BR570.B66   277.1'o8   C82-091270-0

Cover design and illustrations: Niels Wamberg, Denmark.
International edition: ISBN 2-8254-0729-1
Canadian edition—ISBN 0-919599-05-2

© 1982 World Council of Churches
        150 route de Ferney
        1211 Geneva 20, Switzerland.

No. 16 in the Risk Book series

Published in Canada in co-operation with

        Wood Lake Books
        S-6, C-9, R.R.#1
        Winfield BC
        Canada V0H 2C0

Printed & bound in Canada by

        Friesen Printers
        Altona, MB, R0G 0B0
        Canada

To Burton Mack —
who opened my ears to the music of parable song,
and my heart to the presence of the Master Parabler.

TABLE OF CONTENTS

Section I—CANADA AND CANADIANS IN THE 1980s
The Winds of Change

1: *"O Canada, My Home And Native Land..."*
—Assets and Liabilities.................................8

2: *Where Have All the Flowers Gone?*
—Canadian Scenarios for the 1980s...................11

Section II—CANADA DURING THE FIRST WAVE
The Formative Years

1: *In The Beginning (1535-1776)*
—The French and 'Les Anglais'.......................18

2: *Discovering Who We Were Not*
—Canada's Love/Hate Affair With the U.S.A............21

3: *Forging An Identity (1820-1871)*
—Building A Dominion From Sea to Sea...............28

4: *The Land of Promise (1867-1914)*
—Opening the Canadian West.......................39

5: *How We Came Out Of It*
—The Search For the Great Canadian Myth............51

Section III—CANADA DURING THE SECOND WAVE
Changes Subtle and Inexorable

1: *The People Of the Land*
—Canada's Native Inhabitants.......................58

2: *Canada's Churches—Custodians Of the Myth*
—On Trying To Be Both Glue and Yeast...............66

3: *The Nature Of Industrialized Society*
—Beware of Smiling Dragons........................72

4: *What Industrialism Does To People*
—Their Thoughts, Cares and Prayers.................78

5: *How We Came Out Of It*
—Secularism Grows, the Church Declines............81

Section IV—THE THIRD WORD/THIRD WAVE ASSAULT
   Battle Grounds of the Future

   1: *Canadians, Caught in The Crossfire*
      —Watchman, What Of the Night? 90

   2: *Third World Realities and Ambiguities*
      —Life In the Global Village 93

   3: *Third Wave Coming On*
      —The Micro-chip Is Here To Stay 104

   4: *The Collapse Of The Second Wave World*
      —"All The King's Horses..." 109

   5: *First Wave Nostalgia*
      —The Retreat To the Right 111

Section V—THE CHALLENGE FOR THE CHURCHES
   Raft, Wind and Sail

   1: *Some Home Truths About the Canadian Church*
      —A Remnant Pilgrim People 116

   2: Back to Basics
      —New Thoughts on Old Questions 118

   3: *Facing the Apocalypse*
      —How To Sing In The Furnace 123

Notes: 127

Bibliography: 128

Section I

CANADA AND CANADIANS IN THE 1980s

The Winds of Change

1: "O Canada, My Home and Native Land..."

Canada is a large country with a small population. It's the second largest country in the world, but its 25 million inhabitants are only about one-third more than the population of Mexico City.

In some ways the country doesn't make much sense. All of the continent's natural divisions run north and south but the political boundary runs east and west. The vast majority of Canadians live along a narrow corridor within 100 miles of the U.S. border, stretched out for some 5000 miles from the Atlantic Ocean to the Pacific. Furthermore, 40% of that population is packed into one little 600-mile segment of the ribbon between Quebec City and Windsor, Ontario.

Canadians share the North American continent with the United States of America (and Mexico). Not unnaturally, they share many things in common with Americans. But Canadians are *not* Americans. There are very real historical, cultural, socio-political and psychological differences between the two peoples, and the Canadians have fought several bloody wars to remain that way.

My mother, being American and thus subjected to the terrible fate of learning her history only from American textbooks, grew up thinking that the Americans had won the War of 1812. It was only after she married my dad that she discovered Canadians have a rather different view of the matter!

But Canadians are not a particularly self-conscious people, which is both a liability and an asset. I grew up in Canada in a home that experienced a procession of overseas missionaries, international students, and other assorted church-related globe-trotters. To be a "global" Christian was, I assumed, the norm.

For most of my professional life (and in particular the last 15 years as a church broadcaster and journalist) I have been trying to persuade my fellow Canadians that they need to take the rest of the world seriously. I find it much more difficult to write a book inviting that rest of the world to take Canadians with equal seriousness.

Twenty years ago it wouldn't have been so hard. We weren't so aware then of the discrepancies between rich nations and poor, of the widening gap between "First" and "Third" worlds, of the imbalance between haves and have-nots. Nor were the world's Christians then so painfully aware of the almost impenetrable complexity of the principalities and powers of this world and the way in which systemic evil embroils all of us in mutual exploitation of one another.

When one tries to unpack that complexity, no matter which way one goes about it, Canadian Christians still emerge as part of the affluent West, the industrialized North, the over-consuming 10% of the world. I find it much easier to evoke compassion and understanding on behalf of the dispossessed two-thirds of the world's peoples than to ask for the same on behalf of a segment of the materially affluent one-third.

The stated mind-set of the World Council of Churches doesn't make the task any easier. Jacques Matthey expresses the matter very succinctly in his introduction to the Report of the recent WCC Melbourne Conference on Evangelism:

> Wherever people use religious, ideological, economic or other means to organize their lives as if they were their own god and in order to exclude those "outside" from the material and spiritual fruits of God's benediction, they place themselves as the centre. That's where Jesus is *not* to be found. He has moved to the periphery. Witness to the Kingdom of God cannot be faithful today if it is not formulated as Good News to the materially poor. This is today's most scandalous division and every attempt to soften that scandal must be denounced as non-Christian.

How does one presume, in the face of such a mandate, to ask Christians to spend any time at all considering the cares and concerns of those who live on the affluent side of that line of demarcation? When words of judgement are rightfully called for, how does one dare to ask for words of grace and forgiveness as well?

But food in the stomach does not assuage anguish in the soul, and many Christians in Canada are carrying around an incredible load of guilt, simply for being who they are.

When the Good News keeps coming at you as bad news you have either to be a masochist or deeply committed to stay with it. Even the options are ambiguous. Should one leave and engage one's energies somewhere where the battle-lines are more clearly defined? Is the decision to stay and attempt to bloom where one has been planted an opting-in or an opting-out of the struggle?

These are some of the realities with which this small book attempts to deal. It assumes that God has been and is at work in the Canadian church. That church has its own unique history, its particular experience of God, and its own place in the contemporary drama of God's unfolding purpose. God might even have a word or two to share with the rest of His/Her people through that encounter in which S/He has been engaged north of the 49th Parallel.*

It is also possible that we shall all of us discover in the next decade or two that the ecumenical ship is not even a ship. It may be nothing more than a raft, afloat on a very stormy sea. We may even discover that God is Himself tipping us off the edge of the raft! In which case we're going to need all the humility, grace and mutual support we can muster. Fortunately those may be the very gifts we shall find waiting for us as we launch out into the eye of the wind.

---

*Author's Note: The author wishes to acknowledge the validity of the argument for using non-sexist language and has tried to do so in what follows. But in the interests of readability, on those few occasions hereafter when literary conventions call for the use of pronouns in reference to the Almighty, forgiveness is asked for using the traditional form thereof.

2: Where Have All The Flowers Gone?

It is three days after Christmas. A lady marches up to the department store toy counter. "This toy is defective," she announces to the clerk behind the counter. "My husband, my son and I have all tried to assemble it, and it just can't be done!"

The unimpressed clerk, raising one eyebrow, replies, "Madam, there is absolutely nothing wrong with that toy. It is a modern educational toy designed to help your child adjust to the realities of the 1980s world. Any way he tries to put it together—is wrong."

The kid has my sympathies. I'm not too sure about the 1980s either.

I loved the 1960s! The nation's campuses were alive with student unrest. Even our music promised a brave new world ("We shall overcome," "If I had a hammer," etc.). Nowadays the only way to provoke a student revolt would be to increase the price of hamburgers in the college cafeteria. And it's hard to rally the troops around some contemporary country music epic like "Drop-kick me, Jesus, through the goalposts of life"!

Canadians are responding in a variety of ways to the crunch of the 1980s. If you were to dip into the multi-hued currents of contemporary Canadiana, at or near any one of the nation's mainline churches, you might very well encounter at least one of the following scenarios:

The secular humanist

Scene: 5:00 PM, a cocktail lounge, downtown Canada:

"So you work for the church, eh? (Waitress—another round here, please). *Me? ... I went to Sunday School a few times when I was a kid. I went to church once a couple of years ago, but somehow it just didn't give me that "feeling", you know.....*

"You do TV? What kind of shows? ... Oh, those .... Geez, I see those starving refugee kids on the screen and frankly it scares the hell out of me. I think of my own son (here's a picture of him, cute little guy, isn't he? Looks just like his mother). Anyway, the way I figure it—you keep all those starving black kids alive and some day they're going to

come over here and take from my kid the things I'm working really hard to build for him....

"Besides you can't believe everything those refugee organizations tell you. A friend of mine was in Bangladesh once and saw all this wheat we sent just rotting on the dock .... and the money we give? Most of it gets spent right here, keeping the refugee organizations fat and healthy (Thanks miss—keep the change). So I just don't give to any of them.

"When you've got a mortgage, the car and a new kid - and sales way off with this recession—there's not much left out of $30,000 a year to give to things like that. Like, if you were me—and I was going to church and all—with my salary and my commitments, how much should I give? ... $20? ... well-l ... $20 a week!! Oh my God! ...

"Look I've got to be off, got to chair a meeting of the community recreation association tonight ... Hey, nice talking to you ...."

The businessman's lament

Scene: 12:00 Noon, a restaurant, city-centre Canada:

He goes to church every Sunday. Sometimes he flies back early from a business trip so that he won't miss the Sunday service. His church is important to him and last year when the congregation elected him as their lay-delegate to the denomination's annual conference he took three days of his vacation to attend.

Now he's hurt and he's puzzled. There were moments of great inspiration and times of rich fellowship at the conference. It's the resolutions that are bothering him.

"Why?" he complains to his business associate over lunch. "Why is my church so anti-business and so anti-American? They passed resolutions against doing trade with South Africa, against American involvement in Latin America, against the northern pipeline—even against putting defensive missles in Europe! Don't they realize that if we don't defend this nation the Russians will come in and destroy everything we believe in?"

"Maybe now you understand what I've been trying to tell you," responds his luncheon companion. "The church headquarters staff are a bunch of left-wing intellectual radicals. They draft their resolutions and statements in ignorance and issue them as if they were speaking for the whole church. But they never ask us for our input on these issues. There was a bishop disrupted our annual stockholders' meeting last year, raising questions about company investments that had no place on the floor of an annual meeting. To me, it's outright interference on the part of the church. I find it offensive and inappropriate. Then there's that so-called World Council of Churches—totally controlled by Communists and Marxist liberationists ...."

"Well I don't know about all that," interjects our conference delegate. "I just wish they weren't so—well, so righteous about it all."

A burned-out crusader

Scene: Evening in surburban Canada, the phone rings:

"Thursday night for an Action Group on El Salvador? Well, I'd have to miss an executive meeting at the food co-op. Make it next week and I'll shift the Native Concerns Task Force to Monday ..... hold it, sorry, Monday's the congregational Outreach Committee... but what will that matter, I am the Outreach Committee!...."

For 40 years she's been supporting every cause that's come across her pastor's desk—and there have been lots of them. She's fought for the rights of welfare mothers, marched for nuclear disarmament, written letters for Amnesty International, and worked for the election of a dozen different politicians. Now, even though she works full time at her own career, she still gives many of her evenings and most of her weekends to the causes she believes in.

It was easier a few years ago when she was winning a few of the battles. She could believe that her efforts really did make a difference; that she was helping to make a reality of the prayer "Thy Kingdom come on earth ....". But now it's a lonely road with not many victories along the way and she's tired. The moments of crazy hope are getting fewer, replaced by a vacillation between moments of cynicism and despair.

What bothers her the most is trying to keep a foot in so many different camps. Because she tries to remain open to all comers, her radical friends call her a wishy-washy, fence-sitting liberal. The church conservatives, on the other hand, call her a meddlesome do-gooder. The "evangelicals" are praying for her conversion. She sees herself as trying to live a ministry of reconciliation while being faithful to a prophetic calling. "It would be so much easier" she says to herself, "if I didn't have to try to be Christian *about it."*

The homeless radical

Scene: Late afternoon, an inner-city church drop-in centre:

You could legitimately call it holy rage. The frustration is boiling over inside him: "They're stupid! Just stupid!"

He has just come back from a recruiting reception given by an organization of right-wing business and church people. Amongst other things he has asked them to articulate their theological and/or biblical base. Their reply? "Well, we haven't had time to get around to that yet."

"Calling them 'stupid' isn't going to be very helpful," counsel his friends. "You don't change anybody by writing them off." And of course his friends are right.

But nobody else there, either at the reception or amongst his friends, has spent the past month with him, living amongst the peasants of Latin America. He has visited political prisoners in their cells; he has known the hair-raising chill of the military bayonet pointed at your stomach. And now, just this morning has come word that the priest with whom he lived for a week of his Latin American sojourn has been "salvaged." A paramilitary hit squad took him from his crude cabin in the middle of the night. Yesterday the villagers found his body—what was left of it—by the side of the road.

"Is it wrong," he now asks himself, "when you have nowhere else to turn, to take up arms against oppression?"

And what about here? How does one live in the midst of comfort and security knowing that life is a living hell for so many others? How does one communicate what it is really like to those who have never been there?

You seek out a community, one that will hear you and help you to carry the brokenness which you feel. You raise your concerns every way and every place you can. And you pray for compassion to enable you to see the prisons in which the affluent too are confined. Most of all you pray to be free of the bitterness which threatens always to cloud your own vision.

But sometimes it all seems so stupid!

Blessed assurance, Jesus is mine

Scene: Coffee time, a kitchen in small town Canada:

"It's like living out of the pages of the New Testament! You just know that God is real and that He lives in your heart!"

Quite a change I see before me. Gone is the haggard look, gone too the asthma that has plagued her for years. She really has been "born again."

Not that she is new to religion. She grew up in the church. But now there is something new. "It's not something you work *at like before," she observes, "It's more like tapping in to another source of power and letting it flow through you." Twice she has experienced a "gift of tongues" while participating in the weekly prayer and Bible study group that has become her real spiritual home.*

She's dropped a few committees. Not because she's opposed to what they're about but because many of their activities don't seem all that important to her any more. "You can't change the world by political action," she says. "Nor can you bring in the kingdom of love by supporting violence. You have to change the hearts of individuals one at a time. If you do that, you can leave it to God to look after the affairs of the world."

She still supports her church, generously—though she gives less to its mission funds than she used to. That's because she now gives a lot of her money to other mission groups that, to her, preach a more "fundamental" gospel than her own church seems to. She supports several of the TV evangelists; and she too is praying that an experience of spiritual renewal will come to our weary crusader!

Section II

CANADA DURING THE FIRST WAVE

The Formative Years

1: In the Beginning (1535-1776)

Such contemporary vignettes of Canadiana would have seemed like tales from outer space to Fr. Denis Jamay and his three fellow Recollet priests that morning in 1615 when they first viewed the tiny settlement of Quebec. A few wooden buildings, a scattering of Indian dwellings, and mile after mile of endless forest; this was the New France which they had come to claim for God.

The French Huguenot traders who comprised the Company of 100 Associates were not overjoyed at the appearance of Roman Catholic priests in their new colony, but there was a revival afoot in 17th century France which sent some remarkable individuals off to the new world. For instance, Jeanne Mance in response to a religious vision, left Paris in 1641 to participate in the founding of the new colony at Montreal. Her friends were convinced that she was throwing away both life and fortune, but she went anyway and founded some of the first hospitals and schools in New France.

The Jesuits also had a vision for the new world—a model ultramontane church and a state founded on Catholic principles and loyal to the Holy See. When the Jesuits finally gained access to New France they quickly surmised that the rest of the white population was corrupting the Indians faster than the Recollets were converting them. Jesuit policy became one of establishing separate villages for native Christians. At Huronia at the eastern tip of Lake Superior they constructed a model Indian mission, the extent of which archeologists are still uncovering.

Huronia lasted only 10 years, from 1639 to 1649. It became one of the earliest victims of the struggle for furs between the competing European traders and their Indian partners. The Iroquois, armed with guns by the Dutch and British, wiped out the mission. One of the casualties was its leader, Fr. Jean Brebeuf. Brebeuf left behind one of the most beautiful early contextualizations of the Christian gospel in Indian cultural form, the haunting, and in Canada very familiar, Huron Carol.

The Jesuits were not totally to be denied their dream. New France's first bishop, Bishop Laval, neatly took the church in Canada out of French politics by getting himself appointed directly by the Pope rather than the King of France. This action was to prove the salvation of the church in the new world when New France fell to the British in 1759.

By that time Laval and his successors had helped to create a unique culture in the new world. The entire colony was divided up into some 250 seigneuries each with its central manor house, parish church, and surrounding tenant farms. The system, though rooted in old world feudalism, was admirably suited to the needs of a new frontier. It provided the settler farmer with order, protection, social welfare, government and a sense of belonging. It also meant that the French Canadian habitants came in second best to their Yankee cousins in grabbing control of the new world's resources.

The church also took the lead in education, though in French Canada education was constructed along classical lines designed to suit the needs of the church and the landed gentry. Not until Quebec's Quiet Revolution of the 1950s was this model changed.

The Roman Catholic church also became the *de facto* government of the original French settlers in Acadia (Canada's Maritime provinces). When the British finally established a colony in "Canada" (at Halifax in 1749) one of the first acts of that colonial government was to evict the 8,000 Acadians from their land. Although half of the Acadians eventually found their way back, they found that the best of their lands had been taken over by American and British settlers. The expulsion of the Acadians remains to this day one of the tender spots of French/English relations in Canada.

The church heirarchy in Quebec was not blind to what was happening in the Maritimes. And when Halifax's German-speaking Lutherans agreed to worship in English with their Anglican friends, Quebec officials noted that it was not long before the Lutheranism went as well. When the British took over Quebec in 1759 the church was determined not to let a similar fate occur.

It was aided in this determination by Laval's foresight in attaching his see directly to Rome. France left the new world but the French church remained. It now took the lead in the preservation of French culture and language. The British governors, realizing that for the forseeable future they were going to have mainly francophone subjects, worked with the church to establish the basis for the bi-lingual and bi-cultural nature of Canada which still exists.

Bishop Briand, his supply of priests from France cut off by the British takeover, set about training an indigenous clergy. His determination to preserve the language showed itself in the publication, within five years of the British conquest, of the first book ever printed in Canada—a Roman Catholic catechism printed in French.

While the Roman Catholics were adjusting to their dis-establishment as the official church of New France, the Church of England was preparing to step into that role. An Anglican eucharist had been celebrated on Baffin Island as early as 1578 during one of Martin Frobisher's abortive attempts to discover the Northwest Passage. Shortly there-after (in 1583) Sir Humphrey Gilbert had declared the Church of England "established" in the new world, albeit only at his tiny and temporary settlement at St. John's Newfound-land. One of the first acts of that Nova Scotia legislature which expelled the Acadians was the establishing of the English church and the outlawing of Roman Catholicism in the colony!

The Royal Engineers, at the King's direction, constructed St. Paul's Church in Halifax, the Anglican Cathedral in Quebec, and the Cathedral in Montreal. The French had supported their church via a 1/26th tithe on the colony's revenues, but the English decided to set aside land in the new world as "Clergy Reserves." In Upper Canada (Ontario) this amounted to 1/7th of the land and was to prove the single most contentious political issue in the colony. It was to spark the closest thing to a revolution that Canada has yet experienced.

Early attempts at this "establishment" in Britain's new francophone colony were not crowned with success. Even the importation of French-speaking Anglican clergy failed to dent the phalanxes of the Roman Church. As for the mainly-Calvinist anglophone merchants who had moved in after the Conquest, there were events brewing to the south which made them less than eager to pledge allegiance to the Anglican church. Those events were to boil over into a full-blown revolution and result in the establishment of the United States of America.

Canada's Love/Hate Affair with the USA

2: Discovering Who We Were Not (1776-1820)

There were two empty chairs at the table when 13 of Great Britain's American colonies gathered in Philadelphia in the summer of 1774 for the American Continental Congress. Neither Nova Scotia nor Quebec accepted their invitations to participate.

On the surface their absence was puzzling. Nova Scotia was two thirds transplanted New Englanders anyway and there was no reason to expect the Quebecois to harbour feelings of loyalty towards the British.

But deeper down lay some of those fundamental differences between Canadians and Americans. Many Nova Scotians had left New England because they disliked the more extreme republican sentiments brewing there. The recent influxes of Highland and Ulster Presbyterians and Yorkshire Methodists were more intent on establishing their farms than on dumping tea into Boston Harbour. And Halifax, the seat of government, was essentially a British garrison town whose leading citizens were not prepared to run off to Philadelphia to plan a revolution!

In French Canada Bishop Briand had used the American

threat to great advantage, trading francophone loyalty in exchange for legal and linguistic concessions for his people and his church. Given a choice between British benevolent paternalism and American radical republicanism, there was no question where the conservative French church heirarchy was going to side.

Undeterred, the American Fathers of Confederation decided to take the northern colonies by force. In the summer of 1775 they sent an army up the Richelieu River through St. Jean, Montreal, and Trois Rivieres. The arrival of a second American army (under General Benedict Arnold) prompted the launching of a major assault on the fortress of Quebec in the middle of a raging blizzard on the night of 31 December 1775. The invaders were repulsed.

Throughout that winter 4000 American troops laid seige to the city. On 7 May the ice in the St. Lawrence cleared and three British troop ships hove into view. The Americans packed up and went home. Their honour and their Revolution were saved when they soundly defeated the British general who followed them down the Richelieu but they made no further attempts to include the two northern colonies in the Revolutionary War.

The British negotiators at the subsequent Treaty of Versailles treated the northern colonies with a disdain that should have driven them into the revolutionary camp. Nobody bothered to consult the colonials about the terms of the settlement. Not for the first (or indeed the last) time British diplomats were prepared to give Canada away. (At one point during the 1763 negotiations with France it had been a toss-up between keeping the northern colonies or swapping them for the Caribbean island of Guadeloupe!) A huge portion of old Acadia and the southern part of Quebec were ceded to the new republic (to become the present day American State of Maine).

The Loyalist Tide

The most important consequence for Canada came not during but after the Revolutionary War. Many Americans had fought against the republican armies. Some of them were rock-ribbed Tories. Others (like one whole side of my ancestors) were simply farmers and tradesmen who were not at all convinced that life in the new republic was going to be better for them than life under the umbrella of British colonial rule. Now these "Loyalists" were to suffer the same fate as the Acadians.

They were hunted out and humiliated. Some were hanged. Their properties were confiscated. With such goods as they could carry with them they were turned out and told to head north. By the tens of thousands the Loyalists streamed across into Canada. Almost overnight a population of 120,000 had to accommodate an additional 40,000. Some of the newcomers went to the Maritimes but the vast majority headed for the virtually unsettled regions of what is today southern Ontario.

The government out of old military stores provided each family with an axe, a saw, a spade, a hammer and some nails. Every five families shared a gun with which to shoot game and a whipsaw for sawing planks. For the first few years there was assistance with food rations and seed but this ceased in 1787 to be followed by the worst drought and most severe winter of the decade. Without the help of the Indians and each other, many of the settlers would not have survived.

Several million acres of the best shorefront land were already in either crown or clergy reserve (set aside for the state or the church) so the settlers had to take allotments in the second and third ranges back from the river. Getting clear title was a nightmare. There were no mills, no bridges, no open land on which to build a cottage, and no roads. Even if a settler did honour the obligation to construct and maintain a road across his property it would like as not end at land reserved for the clergy or someone in England who had friends at court!

An Established Church?

It was totally inappropriate under such circumstances to attempt to transplant the English parish structure of an Established Church. By now the Church of Scotland had also arrived upon the scene. With some legitimacy these canny Scots claimed that they too were entitled to part of the Clergy Reserves. Undismayed, the new Anglican bishops in Nova Scotia (Bishop Charles Inglis) and Quebec (Bishop Jacob Mountain) set about trying to "establish" the Church of England.

Inglis was the kind of British aristocrat who opposed free seats in the churches because this would make it possible "for men of the worst character to sit down beside the most religious and respectable characters of the parish." Small wonder that his tracts on behalf of the Tory cause while he was rector of New York's Trinity Church had failed to impress American patriots.

Both in the Maritimes and later in Upper Canada the Church of England worked hand in glove with the English governing classes to ensure that higher education remained in the hands of the Established church—thus ensuring that no malicious republican sentiments would be allowed to corrupt the minds of students. Inglis established a college within two years of his arrival in Halifax but he promptly set many of the colony's citizens against him by insisting that all matriculating students sign the Anglican 39 Articles and promise thereafter to attend the Church of England!

Bishop Mountain was never able to mount a similar offensive in Lower Canada (Quebec). He complained bitterly when Briand's successor, playing francophone loyalty off against the second American attempt to invade Canada, won the right to call himself the "Catholic Bishop of Quebec." But there was a more grassroots assault on establishmentarianism taking place in the backwoods of Loyalist Upper Canada. The Methodists were coming into their own.

Methodism was admirably suited to the frontier conditions of Upper Canada. The traditional Methodist class meeting provided a model for lay leadership and consistent religious community. Then there was the Methodist circuit-rider. Throughout the critical years of Upper Canada's development it was the "saddle-bag parsons" who kept the community together. Moving along from cabin to cabin, surviving almost exclusively on the hospitality of each successive settler, they were the couriers of news, the teachers of children, the bringers of spiritual comfort, and ultimately the catalysts for political change.

But first there were the Americans to contend with again.

The War of 1812

One Canadian historian has observed that the War of 1812 was the "foundation war for Upper Canada, the defence of its heritage for Lower, and for the Maritimes, privateering and good times."[1] Certainly it was the newly established Loyalist settlers of Upper Canada who bore the brunt of the conflict.

The main reason for the conflict was simple enough. The hawks in the U.S. Congress saw a chance to grab Florida and Canada while Britain was busy with Napoleon. Thomas Jefferson was of the opinion that victory would be but a "mere matter of marching," and considering that eight million people were taking on less than half a million, it looked as though he was right.

Not all Americans agreed with him. The New Englanders refused to have anything to do with the whole affair, and the American Secretary of Defense wisely observed that the war was unnecessary—give the British colonial office long enough to bungle Canadian affairs and the northerners would soon come knocking on U.S. doors of their own accord!

For all of that it was a bloody war with moments of great barbarity. One December evening the American occupier of Fort George burned the town of Newark to the ground, turning some 400 men, women and children out into the snow. He thereupon retreated to Buffalo where the Canadians found him nine nights later. They bayoneted his entire garrison and burned not only Buffalo but also Black Rock, Lewiston and Fort Schlosser to the ground.

Commodore Perry roamed Lake Erie at will, pillaging Canadian settlements along its shore. One of the most tragic destructions of the war was the wiping out of Moraviantown —a community of Christian Indians which had been established by Moravian missionaries from the USA. The Moravians had followed their Indian friends to Canada when the latter had been expelled from their lands in the American territories.

The Canadians were seriously outnumbered in every one of the battles of this war and might well have lost if it had not been for the Indians and the French Canadians. Tecumseh the Shawnee Chief threw his lot in with the Canadians, and Colonel Charles-Michel de Salaberry turned back an invasion force at Chateauguay that outnumbered his French-Canadian troops five to one.

At one point in the war the Americans burned the Parliament buildings in what is now downtown Toronto. The British completed the ignominy by marching into Washington one August day in 1814. They surprised President Madison in the middle of his supper and proceeded to burn the American parliament buildings—and part of the presidential mansion as well. Fortunately a coat of white paint repaired most of the damage to the President's house (and gave it the name by which it is still known today!). But it is not surprising that not much appears in American textbooks about these parts of the War of 1812!

It probably says something about Canada that not much about the War of 1812 appears in Canadian text-books either. The "right to bear arms" is not a great part of the Canadian mythology. But Canadians do like "Jack the Giant Killer" stories—so perhaps 1812 is buried deeper in their psyches than they like to admit.

When the whole affair was over, the Americans and British sat down to settle their differences. As usual, nobody bothered to consult the Canadians. Although a group of Nova Scotia irregulars had captured several ports in Northern Maine during the conflict, the Treaty gave Maine back to the U.S. (again). Since nobody wanted to acknowledge their role in the affair, the Nova Scotians took back home with them the port taxes which they had dutifully collected during the war. To their credit they eventually built themselves a university with the money.

Similarly on the West Coast. The Americans had hastily constructed a fort at the mouth of the Columbia River in

Oregon just before the war. A British ship quickly captured it, with the result that the British flag flew from San Francisco to the Gulf of Alaska throughout the conflict. But Oregon too was ceded back to the Americans and the border between the two nations established far to the north along the 49th Parallel. Plans for an independent Indian state in the West were also shelved and a fisheries agreement entered into which continues to aggravate relations between Canada and the USA to this day.

In retrospect the American history books may have been right after all. The Americans may not have won the *war* of 1812 but they certainly won the *treaty*! The war left Upper Canada ravaged, but confirmed for Canadians two fundamental facts of life: 1) they were not Americans, and 2) if you have to share your bed with a giant—sleep lightly and hang on tight to your share of the covers!

There were to be further run-ins with the Americans before the century was out. Irish Fenian raiders from the USA plagued the border areas throughout the 1860 s (one of them assassinated one of Canada's Fathers of Confederation). Canada's Prime Minister had almost to force his presence on British/American treaty talks at the end of the American Civil War. The Americans were eager for compensation from the British over the latter's support of the South

in that particular conflict. Some American politicians let it be known that Canada would do just fine as payment—if not the whole thing then perhaps the Northwest, or at least British Columbia.

Sir John A. Macdonald saved his fledgling nation as best he could. But as recently as 1903 Britain caved in to President Teddy Roosevelt's threat to send in the marines unless he got his way in a dispute over the border between Alaska and Canada. Once again Canada was barely consulted. All of which may help non-Canadians to understand why, British North America Act or no, Canadians were determined in 1982 to remove the last vestiges of British Parliamentary control over Canadian affairs and finally patriate the Canadian Constitution.

Now, if only we could figure out how to get control of our economy back from the Americans.....!

Building a Dominion from Sea to Sea

2: Forging an Identity (1820-1871)

The major religious communities in Canada have consistently been the *Roman Catholic, Anglican, Methodist* and *Presbyterian* churches (the latter two since 1925 being for the most part merged into the *United* Church of Canada).

While the Pilgrim Fathers were readying the Mayflower for its famous voyage, the first *Lutheran* services in Canada took place on the cold and lonely shores of Hudson's Bay. Only Capt. Jens Munck and two of his crew survived the scurvy which decimated his ice-bound exploration party during that winter of 1619. When spring came the three half-dead men, in a magnificent feat of seamanship, sailed their ship back home to Denmark.

It was more than a century before Lutheranism reappeared in Canada in Nova Scotia's Lunenberg County. Many German troops fought for the British in the American War of Independence. Together with German-speaking settlers who chose not to be part of the republican venture they joined the Loyalist flood into Canada during the 1780s. They were joined 20 years later by a second wave of German-speaking immigrants from Pennsylvania. This latter group, which contained many *Mennonites* and *Brethren*, settled in Ontario's Kitchener/Waterloo area, where their presence is still much in evidence.

It was difficult for Canada's Lutherans to get either funds or pastors. Many of them simply became anglicized and joined the Anglicans or the Methodists. Then one day in 1849 an old man turned up at the annual meeting of the Pittsburgh Synod of the Lutheran Church. Adam Keffer had walked 250 miles to beg for an English-speaking Lutheran pastor for the folks back home near Markham, Ontario. The Synod was understandably impressed but nothing came of it. So the next year old Adam walked the 500-mile round trip again! This time a young Lutheran pastor responded to the call. Shortly thereafter was formed the first Lutheran Synod in Canada, but the Lutheran Church is still trying to forge a distinctly Canadian union out of the disparate European and American strands through which it still operates in Canada. Hopefully the 1980s will see a Canadian merger taking place.

The *Baptists* and *Congregationalists* came to Canada's Maritime provinces with the New Englanders who settled there after the expulsion of the Acadians. It was the issue of higher education which finally galvanized the Baptists into political activity. They were determined to provide an education for their sons and daughters; they would not have them become Anglicans in order to get it. So they established their own university and thereby set the pattern for the subsequent development of higher education in Canada. Throughout the nation's formative years it was the church denominations which established, funded, and for many years operated, the nation's colleges and universities.

The Congregationalists in the Maritimes were seriously hampered by their close identification with the Americans and were shredded by a charismatic revival which swept through Nova Scotia. Congregationalism came back to both Upper and Lower Canada with the Loyalist tide and, with support from the London Missionary Society, did exercise an important influence, particularly in Canada's growing urban centres. However, by the time they came into the 1925 union which created the United Church of Canada, the Congregationalists comprised less than 0.5% of the Canadian population.

The *Disciples of Christ* appeared in Canada early in the 19th century. Never large in number, they did have their own seminary for a time and were major participants in an abortive attempt at a broader church union with the United and Anglican churches in the late 1960s.

The *Quakers* were granted liberty of conscience in Canada even before the American Revolution; so many of them came north when the war broke out. There have never been more than about 7000 Quakers in Canada, but they nevertheless continue to make a contribution to Canadian society far in excess of their numerical strength.

Holiness movements of one kind or another have always kept a streak of Puritanism alive in the Canadian religious mix. American revivalism first spilled over into Canada in Henry Alline's "New Light" revival in Nova Scotia in 1775 and the Methodists made the annual "Camp Meeting" a major feature of their church life. Later, Western Canada was to grow its own particular brand of evangelical fundamentalism and in the 1970s charismatic renewal movements appeared in many of the mainline churches.

Roman Catholicism and the Rebellions

At the conclusion of the War of 1812 the position of the Roman Catholic church in Canada was relatively secure. Bishop Plessis had won for himself a seat in the Lower Canada Legislative Council and even an agreement from the

British to pay part of his salary! His auxiliary, Bishop Macdonnell, was given a seat in the Upper Canada Legislative Council and proceeded by virtue of much tact and diplomacy to ease the way for the growing numbers of non French-speaking Roman Catholics who were moving into that predominantly Protestant colony.

It was the Irish who gave Bishop Plessis his major problem. They flooded into Canada after the potato famines of the 1840s in Ireland. In one peak year (1847) 55,000 poverty-stricken, starving Irish peasants were shipped off to Canada by their English landlords. Half of them died en route or at the Grosse Isle quarantine station down river from Quebec. Those that managed to struggle on to find new homesteads brought with them the epidemics of typhus and cholera which had wrought such havoc on board ship. Along with dispossessed Scottish crofters and the new wave of American immigrants they brought a new and often bitterly anti-British element into Canadian politics.

In Nova Scotia Edmund Burke, a fiery Irish missonary, pulled a leaf out of Bishop Laval's book and went over Plessis' head directly to the Pope to get himself appointed Roman Catholic Bishop of Nova Scotia. Differences between the Irish and the French branches of the Roman Catholic Church in Canada have made for some lively ecclesiastical debates ever since.

Despite Plessis' best efforts it soon became evident that francophones were becoming a minority in Canada. At the outbreak of the American Revolution they had numbered some 103,000 to the English 17,000. In a matter of decades the scales had tipped the other way. Understandably the French church pulled in upon itself. It entered into a conservative, ultramontane and ascetic stance which met not at all the needs of the new breed of French political activists like Louis Joseph Papineau.

Not all of the French Canadians had retreated quietly to their farms while 'Les Anglais' took over the country. With increasing bitterness French politicians watched as English land companies and non French-speaking settlers took over what they regarded to be their homeland.

Events came to a head in December of 1837 when the Lower Canada Rebellion broke out at St. Eustache, north of Montreal. It wasn't much of a fight. Papineau was a better orator than he was an organizer and the rebellion was short-lived. The Roman Catholic heirarchy remained firmly on the side of law and order, thus earning itself the subsequent distrust of future generations of French-Canadian nationalists. The heirarchy was probably right in its reading of the situation. To have supported Papineau's rhetoric and inadequate organization would have invited a retaliation which could only result in the anglicization of both church and province.

But being "right" is sometimes poor compensation for appearing not to be.

The Protestants and the Rebellions

The Rebellion in Upper Canada broke out in the same year and month as its Lower Canada counterpart, but issues of Church and State were much more directly at stake. It too was short-lived and in many ways equally a failure. Its leader, newspaper publisher William Lyon Mackenzie, was also a better orator than organizer.

Underlying the unrest were three fundamental issues. One was political—a growing frustration in people who found themselves shut out of the political process. A second revolved around the total inadequacy of the educational facilities. The third, and the one which most galvanized popular support for the reformers, had to do with questions of religious liberty. At the centre of all three problems was the Family Compact, an informal but impenetrable coalition of English church, aristocracy and money.

The Methodists fired some of the opening salvos. Bishop Mountain was not pleased. He complained to his colleagues in Britain that "the itinerant and mendicant Methodists" were "a set of ignorant Enthusiasts" whose preaching could not help but "perplex the understanding, corrupt the morals, ... relax the nerves of industry, and dissolve the bands of Society."[2] Archdeacon Strachan, the Church of England's champion in Upper Canada, was equally uncomplimentary in his observations.

Young Egerton Ryerson took on the Archdeacon in a newspaper editorial that set the colony on its ear. (His father, loyalist and staunch Anglican, was not pleased. But Colonel Joseph Ryerson was no match for his wife's biblical zeal. In the end he lost all five of his sons to the Methodist ministry!)

The 22-year old cleric was soon writing for Mackenzie's reformist paper but within four years the Methodists had started their own journal, *The Christian Guardian,* and appointed him its editor.

At the start of the 1830s Methodism in British North America ranked fourth in size (70,000 to the Presbyterians' 102,000, The Anglicans' 119,000 and the Roman Catholics' 483,000). Within 20 years it had vaulted into second place to become the largest Protestant church in the land. It had its share of internal disputes between its British, Irish, American and Canadian wings. Internal relations were not improved when the Wesleyan Methodists were able to exploit their ties with the Church of England to secure a portion of the income from the Clergy Reserves. Even Ryerson got caught in this web, with the result that the *Guardian* withheld its support from Mackenzie's uprising.

Mackenzie and Strachan, both Scots, the one Liberal and the other Tory, went at each other hammer and tongs. The latter held firm to his convictions that only Anglican clergy should have the right to perform marriages, that education should remain the preserve of the Church of England, and that the Clergy Reserves were therefore rightfully his.

The failure of the 1837 Rebellion was a great victory for Strachan and the Family Compact. He was made a bishop, and from the Tory homeland funds poured into the diocesan coffers. But the problems over the Clergy Reserves would not go away. Finally, in 1854, the Canadian Parliament simply abolished the reserves altogether and placed all of Canada's religious denominations on an equal footing in the eyes of the law.

The two rebellions were different. The first was a nationalist struggle, the second a class struggle. But two rebellions in one year was too much even for the British to ignore.

They sent Lord Durham to the colonies to find out what was wrong. Durham wasted no time. Concluding that bad government was the underlying problem, he urged the British Parliament to grant responsible, representative government to the colonies, to unite them, and to anglicize them.

In 1841 an Act of Union was duly passed by the British Commons. The results were disastrous. French Canada has never forgiven Durham his obvious intention of eradicating its culture. English and French factions in the new legislature proceeded to checkmate each other through a series of coalition governments. At one point the supposedly unified colony went through ten different governments in as many years! By now there were four separate crown colonies in the Maritimes—Nova Scotia, New Brunswick, Prince Edward Island, and Newfoundland. These viewed developments in Canada West and Canada East with considerable dismay. When an invitation finally came from the senior colony to join in a broader Confederation, the Maritimes could be forgiven for viewing it as a desperation move, anything to break the deadlock!

Evolving Educational Systems

The Act of Union had brought to the fore the fact that Upper and Lower Canada had very different philosophies of education. Combining the French classical system with the more pragmatic educational concerns of Upper Canada's Protestants was an almost impossible task. Egerton Ryerson was now Superintendent of Education for Canada West where he proceeded to design an integrated school system which covered everything from elementary school to teacher training. In Canada East Jean Baptiste Meilleur designed a system which allowed for separate school systems for Protestants and Catholics.

The systems which Ryerson and Meilleur developed completely undid Durham's intention of evolving a unified, unilingual, unicultural, English-speaking colony. Both Ontario and Quebec ultimately evolved educational systems which preserved minority linguistic, cultural and religious rights. In the process they established the precedent that education should be a provincial rather than a federal concern in Canada. This opened the way for Manitoba, later in the same century, to do violence to the language rights of its francophone citizens and for Quebec in more recent times to do the same to its anglophones.

Minority Rights

There was one group in Canada East that did not fit neatly into Meilleur's system: a continuing cluster of French-speaking Protestants. These found themselves in a similar bind to the German-speaking Lutherans in Halifax. For the French Protestants the choice was "keep your faith and lose your language, or keep your language and lose your faith."

Within five years of each other, two remarkable Swiss Protestant women arrived in Canada and addressed themselves to this problem. In 1835 Madame Henrietta Feller established the Grande Ligne Mission and Feller Institute in Quebec's Eastern Townships. Aligning herself with the Baptists, Madame Feller offered schooling and residential care to Francophone Protestant children. Then in 1841, Madame Daniel Amaron set up a second French Protestant language school at Pointe-Aux-Trembles in Montreal's east end. That school eventually became the responsibility of the United Church of Canada which, along with the other mainline Protestant denominations, continues a French-language work to this day. At its peak the French Protestant work had three residential schools, fourteen day schools, and 70 French-speaking pastors.

Today there are some 85,000 French-speaking Protestants in Canada. Francophone Fellowship Baptist and Pentecostal churches have appeared in La Belle Province, fuelled by a charismatic movement within the Roman Catholic church there. The Jehovah's Witnesses have also made strong inroads in Quebec.

Concern for minority rights found another expression during these turbulent years. Some of Nova Scotia's early settlers brought slaves with them, but slavery was abolished in Canada in 1789, just at the conclusion of the American Revolution. Soon Canada became the terminus of an underground railway ferrying runaway negro slaves out of the USA. Many came to Halifax, others settled in Upper Canada around Windsor, Dresden, and Niagara Falls. The trickle turned to a steady stream when the U.S. Congress passed the Fugitive Slave Law in 1850.

Almost every one of Canada's churches undertook to assist the runaways. Some American churches (eg: the Baptists) channelled funds to their Canadian counterparts to aid in settling the fugitives in Canada. Quakers, Moravians, Presbyterians, Methodists and Anglicans, all played a part until the conclusion of the American Civil War in 1865 turned the flow back down to a trickle.

Canada's new black citizens did not automatically find equality, liberty and fraternity in their new homeland. Racism is subtler than that. But their life in Canada was a considerable improvement on that which they had left behind and many of them stayed to make important contributions to Canadian life.

Maturing Churches

The 1840s saw Canadian churches enter actively into the international missionary movement. The needs of the country's own Western frontier absorbed most of the mission energy of the Canadian churches, but in 1844 the Baptists sent Richard Burpee and his wife to Burma. Not to be outdone the Presbyterians shortly thereafter sent John Geddie and his wife to the New Hebrides to found a mission.

Concern for "lost souls" at home spurred the Canadian churches to efforts in the field of temperance legislation. "Toronto the Good" (as Montrealers derisively used to refer to it) was not so virtuous during most of the 19th century. Everywhere in Canada in those days liquor was as common as water and almost as cheap. Taverns abounded. A quart of beer cost five cents and a shot of rum, two. In 1861 there were 70 distilleries and 138 breweries in Canada West, most of them in and around Toronto.

At their camp meetings the Methodists tore into the vices of the liquor trade with a ferocity usually reserved for Satan himself. The Baptists willingly joined in. In the end the crusaders were surprisingly successful. Temperance laws were enacted in many parts of the emerging nation with the consequence that Canada was a relatively 'sober' nation throughout the first half of the 20th century. Some prairie settlements (eg: Saskatoon) were actually founded specifically on temperance principles.

As the nation struggled towards unity, the churches too began to settle their differences. Frontier conditions had shown the irrationality of continuing in the new world disputes which were essentially grounded in the old. Cooperation between denominations was slowly evidencing itself. For instance, when Edgerton Ryerson went to Peterborough one night in 1839 to encourage its Methodists to support their new academy at Cobourg, it was the Scottish Presbyterians who provided the hall (on the initiative perhaps of the Baptist clergyman who was serving as their interim pastor).

It was not until 1955 that Canada's Anglicans changed their name from "The Church of England in Canada" to "The Anglican Church of Canada." However, even before the 1837 rebellions the new Anglican bishop in Quebec was urging that his church become self-supporting. And once the matter of the Clergy Reserves was finally disposed of, the Anglican Church in Canada took hold of its own destiny. In 1857 it established self-governing dioceses. Shortly thereafter the Queen paved the way for the election of a Canadian Primate and the British parliament formally renounced any further "interference" in the affairs of the Canadian church.

The Presbyterians were close to a common Canadian structure by 1850 but the eruption of the Free Church movement in Scotland spilled over into Canada and delayed the formation of one Presbyterian Church in Canada for another 25 years. The Methodists finally reconciled their quarrelling British and American factions at about the same time (1874) but it took another ten years to bring their sectarian splinter groups into one Methodist Church in Canada.

The Baptist form of church government was not conducive to the forming of larger unions, a factor which hampered their participation in the 'churching' of the Canadian West. In 1944 they created a nation-wide federation, though their real strength still resides in individual congregations.

The Road to Confederation

While the churches were working at their internal unity, the nation itself was moving in that direction. The country's 380 "noisy little newspapers" provided the populace with a running commentary on the events of 1864 as John A. Macdonald, Georges-Etienne Cartier (one of Papineau's original band), George Brown (editor of the *Toronto Globe*), D'Arcy McGee and the other Fathers of Confederation met in Charlottetown, Prince Edward Island, to discuss the idea of a Canadian Confederation, a "Dominion From Sea to Sea."

It was an incredible party. The horse-trading continued on through Halifax and St. John, New Brunswick. In the fall the conference moved to Quebec and Montreal; then to Ottawa, winding up in Toronto that November. How is a nation born? "It was the growth of an atmosphere among a few men, a shared experience, a contagious dream, an idea that took hold of different men at different times .... at the 5th glass of champagne .... the 16th oyster .... the 350th blazing torch .... the 4,000th mile ... the 10,000th cheering voice."[3] Whatever, the inspiration took hold.

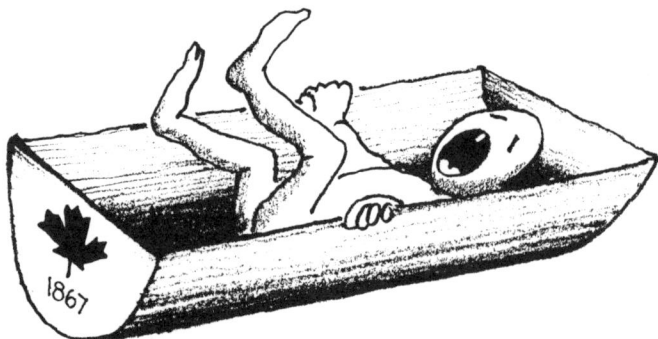

The British North America Act passed the British Parliament in March of 1867 with hardly a ripple of debate. On July 1st, 1867 the Dominion of Canada was born, to the accompaniment of saluting cannon in Ottawa—and yards of black crepe in Halifax.

The infant was alive—barely.

Opening the Canadian West

4: The Land of Promise (1867-1914)

Some Canadian historians have declared that Macdonald's coalition government would not have survived its first testing at the polls had it not been for the support it received from the nation's religious leaders.[4] Nova Scotia's Roman Catholic Archbishop, Thomas Connolly, and his Presbyterian colleague, Dr. George Grant, risked considerable public displeasure by supporting the union. In Quebec, Cartier's friend, Archbishop Baillargeon, enlisted his fellow bishops in a condemnation of those francophone radicals who now sought to disrupt the confederation. In Ontario Edgerton Ryerson wrote a major election pamphlet for the Macdonald/Cartier coalition.

Still, the issue of religious education and separate schools almost tore the flimsy fabric of Confederation apart. New Brunswick passed a "Free School Act" which deeply offended the Catholics. When Cartier, for what he felt to be sound political reasons, advised against forcing the issue, the ultramontane conservatives in the Quebec church were incensed. Armed with the Pope's latest pronouncements against liberalism, Bishop Bourget donned his "Moral

Majority" colours and led his priests into the political fray.

Wilfred Laurier, one of French Canada's brightest young political figures, undertook to head the bishop off. He pointed out that the formation of a separate Catholic political party would invite the formation of a counter-balancing Protestant party, thus effectively dividing the province and ultimately the nation along religious lines. A grateful Canada rewarded Laurier by making him Prime Minister.

Go West, Young Man!

Having survived infancy the young nation turned its attention westward. In 1610, while Samuel de Champlain was busy constructing the first log house at Quebec, the English explorer Henry Hudson was probing through the Artic icepack, looking for the elusive Northwest Passage to the Orient. The Orient he did not find, but by the middle of the century French and English fur-traders were pushing into the interior of the vast continent bordering on the body of water to which he lent his name. Finally in 1670 the British crown chartered the famous Hudson's Bay Company, and exploration of the Canadian West began in earnest.

There followed a century of conflict between the rival trading nations. The British built the most trading posts but the French, at least initially, stamped their language and culture on the West. French traders freely intermingled with the Plains Indians, with the result that a sturdy breed of mixed-blood Metis developed. When the French traders departed the scene their place was taken by the Scots, whose Montreal-based North West Fur Company was far more aggressive and even unscrupulous in its pursuit of furs than ever the French had been.

As the 19th Century dawned, isolated trading posts dotted the prairie landscape from Winnipeg to Fort McLeod. On the other side of the Rockies, Captain James Cook (with both William Bligh and George Vancouver amongst his crew) had arrived at Nootka Sound on Vancouver Island in the year 1778, but Russian and Spanish traders continued to carry on the bulk of the trade with the Indian nations established there. In 1793 Cook's colleague George

Vancouver returned to map the British Columbia coastline. In one of those coincidences of history, that same summer Alexander MacKenzie was exploring overland for the North West Company. MacKenzie became the first European to traverse the Rocky Mountains but he reached the Pacific Coast at Bella Coola only to discover that Vancouver's boats had been there just seven weeks previous!

Capt. Vancouver discovered the site of the city which now bears his name though he missed the mighty river that flows past it on the south. It was Simon Fraser, exploring for the North West Company some 15 years later, who came down the river from inland and gave it its name. Still it was to be another 20 years (1827) before the Hudson's Bay Company undertook to establish a post at Fort Langley—making it the first permanent European settlement on Canada's west coast.

The Red River Settlement

The first sign which the Indian and Metis of the Canadian West had that they were in for some serious competition for their land, was the establishing in 1812 of Manitoba's Selkirk Settlement. Lord Selkirk was an unusual aristocrat. He spent vast sums of his own money establishing displaced Scottish crofters in the new world. Eight hundred of these penniless Scots he settled in Prince Edward Island. For the rest he secured a tract of land from the Hudson's Bay Company along the banks of the Red River in what is today Manitoba.

The North West Company and its Metis allies were less than pleased to find these settlers athwart their trade routes. Selkirk was forced to hire mercenaries (most of whom turned out to be German and French-speaking Roman Catholics) to defend his Gaelic-speaking Presbyterian colonists.

In 1821 the two fur companies "buried the hatchet" in a trade merger and peace descended upon the prairies. Selkirk was able to persuade Fr. Joseph Provencher to come to his settlement to care for the needs of the francophone mercenaries and Metis. When no Gaelic-speaking clergy stepped forward, Selkirk accepted the services of an Anglican, Rev. John West, to minister to the settlers' spiritual needs.

West immediately began developing strategies to meet the needs of the region's native population. He pioneered the Indian Residential School, once widely acclaimed but now seriously criticized by Indian leaders. In retrospect it is easy to criticize West's model. It did remove Indian children from their homes, their culture and their environment at a very vulnerable age. Indian leaders now say that the schools broke up families and effected cultural genocide on the Indian people. But West, in his own way, was attempting to equip the next generation of Indians to deal with a cultural onslaught which he knew was going to be both inevitable and devastating.

One Indian leader put it this way at a recent church conference: "The Church made a lot of mistakes. But when you get right down to it, who else gave a damn about Indians?"

Missionary Action

The end to the fur-trading wars brought an upsurge in missionary activity in the West. The very next year (1822) Provencher persuaded the Oblate Fathers to serve the area. That same year the Anglican Church Missionary Society in Great Britain committed itself to the native peoples of the Northwest. Then the Hudson's Bay Company invited the Methodists to begin work amongst the Cree Indians.

Some incredible tales are told about those early missionaries. For instance, Rev. William Bompas, from his base in Fort Simpson, served a pastoral charge that covered more than a million square miles. He visited most of it too. A quarter of a century after he had departed the scene, an American Episcopal bishop in Alaska found a group of Christian Indians who were still dutifully praying for Queen Victoria! Bompas was obviously no respecter of political boundaries!

The Oblate Father Lacombe, and the Methodists Rundle and McDougall, were instrumental in negotiating peace treaties between several warring Indian tribes. They also made possible negotiations between Alberta's Indians and the Canadian Pacific Railway without which a "whites vs. Indians" war would have been inevitable.

As it was, the Canadian west was never to be the "Wild West" experienced south of the border. There were no Indian massacres, no Cavalry charges. When the famed North West Mounted Police took over in 1874, they were able to maintain peace throughout the West with relative ease. It was a tribute, in large part, to the fact that the missionaries had been there first.

Both the Anglicans and the Methodists were eager to ordain a native clergy. The objective was made easier thanks to the efforts of James Evans who pioneered the Methodist work at Norway House. Evans not only invented an alphabet for the Cree language and proceeded to translate hymns and Scripture portions, he also made himself a printing press out of old tea chests, blocks of wood, and a discarded fur-baling press. With ink made from soot and fish oil, and with strips of birchbark for paper, he went into the printing business! Unfortunately, the Hudson's Bay Company disliked Evans' uncompromising stands against Sabbath work and the liquor trade. They trumped up charges against him and he was recalled to England where he died shortly after—though not before the Company admitted that their charges against him were a total fabrication.

The Presbyterians were late getting into the act. It was not until 1851 that they finally found a Gaelic-speaking minister for the Selkirk settlers. But once he got there, Rev. John Black stayed for the next 30 years. Making up for lost time the settlers raised $500 between them and sent one of their number, James Nisbet, off to evangelize the West! Nisbet set up a mission house, a church and a school, and thus founded Prince Albert, Saskatchewan.

British Columbia

In 1836 as Papineau and Mackenzie were preparing their rebellions, 3000 miles away on the B.C. Coast the Hudson's Bay Company had more important things on its mind. It had just put into service its little coastal steamer, the "S.S. Beaver." Anglican and Roman Catholic missionaries followed close in its wake and began work amongst the coastal Indians.

In 1843 the Company added another trading fort at Victoria, on Vancouver Island, which proceeded in six short years to blossom into a crown colony. When gold was discovered in the Cariboo 14 years later, the B.C. mainland also became a crown colony and the boom was on.

The churches in the East heard the call of this new frontier. Modern travel posters declare that "Getting There Is Half the Fun." This was hardly the case for the four Methodist clergy who volunteered to go. First they headed off to New York by train. From there they shipped to Panama, transhipped to San Francisco, and finally took a sailing packet to Victoria. They preached in bar-rooms, rooming houses, and on the street-corners. B.C. was wide open. Boom towns like Barkerville lured gold-seekers by the thousands. The only viable way to get to the gold was up the canyon of the Fraser River, where in places the famous Cariboo Road literally hung from wooden pegs driven into the rock face of the canyon walls. You had to have a lot of faith or a lot of greed to risk the trip.

The white man's onslaught devastated a centuries-old native civilization. It also brought an epidemic of smallpox that in 1862 wiped out entire Indian villages. Missionaries like William Duncan and Thomas Crosby worked diligently, providing some of the first schools and hospitals anywhere on the coast. But like the rest of Canada's native populations, B.C.'s Indians were simply overwhelmed by the sheer magnitude of the cultural invasion.

By 1866, with the gold-fields playing out and a restless southern neighbour casting covetous eyes northward, the two west coast colonies were amalgamated. They then cast about to find an acceptable suitor for their hand in marriage. They found him alive, reasonably well, and living in Ottawa.

Manitoba

About this time the Red River settlers and their Metis neighbours woke up to the fact that they were not even going to be consulted about a possible marriage. The banns had already been published! A Canadian government survey party was already laying out a road from Fort Garry on the Red River to Fort William at the head of Lake Superior. On December 1 1868 the wedding dowries were exchanged. Canada paid $1,500,000 to the Hudson's Bay Company. In return it got the prairies, the Northwest Territories, half of Baffin Island, and all of the Eastern Arctic!

The Selkirk settlers didn't mind all that much but the Metis were deeply concerned. Already a trickle of Ontario farmers was moving in, taking over traditional Metis and Indian hunting grounds. That summer Louis Riel returned from seminary in Montreal and proceeded to organize his fellow Metis. They formed a council, took over Fort Garry without firing a shot, elected a legislative assembly and drafted a Bill of Rights. The Canadian government sent Donald Smith, the respected Hudson's Bay Company Governor, to Fort Garry to negotiate with Riel. All was going well until there happened one of those crazy incidents that change the course of history.

Among the road builders was an Irish Protestant hothead named Thomas Scott. Before Smith and Riel could complete their negotiations, Scott attempted to overthrow Riel by force. Reacting with equal impetuosity, Riel put Scott before a firing squad. This was too much for the pride of English Canada and the Loyal Orange Order! Twelve thousand troops (half again as many as the entire force with which the Canadians had stood up to the Americans during the War of 1812) were dispatched to the prairies to put the Metis, the Indians, and the French in their place. Eventually Riel was hanged, and in 1870 the province of Manitoba joined Canadian Confederation.

Understandably Louis Riel has become a folk hero for Canada's native and French minorities. The failure of the Roman Catholic church to throw its support behind him was bitterly resented both in the West and in Quebec. French culture on the prairies survived, but only in isolated pockets. The boom years for Canada had begun.

The Boom Years

It was the railroad that made it all possible. The transcontinental line was part of the marriage contract negotiated by British Columbia when it entered the Confederation. When it was built the Canadian Pacific Railroad was the longest railroad in the world. It almost bankrupted the nation. It was shored up by government land grants, loans and outright gifts of cash, but without it there would have been no nation.

By 1881 the railroad reached Winnipeg and from there the track-layers raced across the open prairie laying as many as three miles of track in a single day. The Rockies were a different story. It took four more years before the tracks from east and west met near Revelstoke, B.C.

Then the settlers came. From every part of Europe, from America, from Asia. In the 15 years between 1896 and 1911 Canada's population jumped from five million to eight million. People sold 12-room houses in England to "make their fortune" in prairie wheat. Others left peasant cottages on the Russian steppes to take up the promise of free land in a new world. "The opportunity of free land, of course. That's why most settlers came. All the rest of the world seemed to be gone, the world we knew. Ten dollars got you started and ten dollars was awfully cheap for 160 acres of your choice. There was no bargain like it!"[5]

Many of the new immigrants hadn't the faintest idea about farming. More than one returned penniless to the old country, defeated by the harsh Canadian winters and successive crop failures. At the start it was a terribly lonely existence, especially for the women. One pioneer describes her arrival in the middle of nowhere. Finally they found a man with a wagon who agreed to drive them out to pick a homestead. "South, north, east or west?" he asked. They chose north. About three miles out, the man stopped the wagon, swept his arm and said, "Take your pick, the choice is yours." A quarter-section chosen, they unloaded the wagon. Then, as she says, recovering her manners she got out her little primus stove, "... right there on the bald-headed prairie, put it behind a box for a windbreak and in about 15 minutes we had a little tea party going. Tea, biscuits, butter and strawberry jam."

The tea over, her husband quickly threw up the tent, gave her his rifle, and headed off to file his claim at the town two days' journey away. Before he left, their new friend quickly garnered a pile of dried brown material lying around on the ground: "Buffalo chips, ma'am—burn 'em instead of that little primus." Then the two men were gone.

"There I was with my two children, Peg and James, hand in hand, looking rather forlorn, I must say. Then the wagon was gone, hidden by a dip in the land, and there I was with my two children alone in a new land. Me and my children, my tent and my English biscuits, and surrounded by buffalo chips..." [6]

As the settlers followed the railroad west, little villages

sprang up along the rail line. With the villages came the church. Another pioneer remembers what it was like, moving from place to place, always looking for a better piece of land or the perfect location. "It was never a question of land running out," he recalls. "You'd go into a new place... My dad would go into town and shake hands with the livery-barn man—he was the one you got to know. Before you knew it, dad would have met four or five other farmers hanging around in the little office. Mother would want to know where the church was. We were Presbyterian. We'd all go to church the first Sunday and the visiting minister—always a visiting minister unless it was a town church— he'd announce from the pulpit who we were. After church, out in the yard, mother and dad would meet the neighbours, the sewing circle, the Ladies Aid or whatever it was in those days. In ten minutes we'd be playing with children our own age in the churchyard and next week we'd be visiting each other. That's the way it worked."[7]

Some of the settlers came in groups and brought their churches with them. Icelanders, Ukrainians, Norwegians and Poles, they scattered ethnic settlements across the prairie landscape. From Russia came German-speaking Mennonites and Russian-speaking Doukhobors—both on the promise that Canada would respect their pacifist principles (a promise put sorely to the test during two subsequent world wars).

At one point the Doukhobors severely tried the patience of their Mennonite neighbours. Orthodox Doukhobors will not eat meat or slaughter animals but the pesky prairie gophers were riddling their wheat fields with burrows. The Doukhobors solved the dilemma by trapping the gophers, transporting them across the river, and "giving" them to the Mennonites!

After the First World War, Hutterites from the USA brought their style of communal living to the western prairies where they now number more than 10,000 persons in some 50 thriving colonies.

In many prairie communities the onion-spire of an Orthodox church is as much a part of the sky-line as the grain elevator. Part of the immigration at the turn of the century, the

Ukrainians brought a distinctive culture and a mixture of Orthodox loyalties into the Canadian religious mix.

Church Union

Distances are vast on the prairies and neighbours important. As nationalities and cultures intermingled, religious differences seemed to be less important. And as the difficulties of "churching" the Western frontier impressed themselves ever more strongly upon church leaders in the East, pressure there began to mount for some means of reducing competition between the churches. The more far-sighted of the churches' leaders became aware that the winds of God were about to rend the sails of some cherished denominational vessels.

There was a growing concern for the problems of Canada's urban populations as well. The Salvation Army had brought its unique ministry to Canada in 1881, and out of the nation's new universities were emerging churchmen who questioned the conservatism of traditional theology. They asked about the rights of immigrant workers in the Fort William coal yards, about night school classes for working girls in Toronto, about mission houses in the slums of Montreal. The new liberalism was countered by some powerful old-line churchmen, and the familiar debates thundered through the halls of many a church conference: Genesis vs. Evolution, Biblical Literalism vs. Textual Criticism, Orthodoxy vs. the Social Gospel. As the theological issues sought their resolution, the question of church union began also to arise.

The Presbyterians had been the first to get their own house in order, with the very sensible attitude that Canada's future was more important than Scotland's past. So it was appropriate that the proposal that actually triggered church union should be made by a Presbyterian, the official observer to the Methodist Quadrennial Conference in Winnipeg in 1902. The Methodists responded enthusiastically to the idea of a merger between Presbyterians, Methodists and Congregationalists. Six years later a Joint Union Committee had come up with a Plan of Union which critics observed contained "a harmony of views but a minimum of credal novelty!'' Still it was a masterful weaving together of distinctive Christian traditions and differing forms of ecclesiastical organization.

By 1912 the ruling bodies of all three churches had approved the Plan, and union seemed imminent. But Presbyterian polity called for a remit to the presbyteries and congregations. When one-third of these showed opposition to the Union, the Presbyterian General Assembly asked its partner churches to defer action until it could bridge its own internal divisions.

Meanwhile all across Canada, and particularily on the prairies, congregations in local communities were simply going ahead with church union based on the 1908 Plan. Each time there was a deferral of action a new rash of community churches broke out, so that by the time the Union was achieved in 1925 there were more than 1000 local union congregations across the land. At the eleventh hour the Anglicans came back from a Lambeth Conference eager to join in union talks, but the Presbyterian minority was becoming so determined that the leadership of the three already committed churches decided that to prolong discussions would be to invite a stalemate. As it was, the voting in Ontario (where resided most of the population and whence came most of the mission funds) came out almost 50/50. Fortunately for the pro-Unionists the rest of the country was strongly in favour, with the result that the balance over-all came out about ¾ for and ¼ against.

Not since the issue of the Clergy Reserves and the separate schools had the nation's churches caused such a furore in Canadian legislatures. There were bills to be passed through each of the provincial legislative assemblies. In the federal parliament the Prime Minister (Mackenzie King) was Presbyterian and firmly opposed to Church Union. It took the eloquence of Arthur Meighen, the Leader of the Opposition, to carry the day, with the result that on 10 June, 1925 the new United Church of Canada was born. And that night the ''Continuing'' Presbyterian Church in Canada met in session of its own.

It took more than ten years to sort out relations between

the new United Church and the third of Canada's Presbyterians who chose not to side with their General Assembly. When I was a student at the old Presbyterian College in Montreal, the floor boards in the hall still creaked from the night the anti-Unionists threw the pro-Unionist theologs out of residence. The ousted seminarians came back in through a window, unreeled the fire hoses and went looking for revenge! Hardly a dignified theological discussion.

The United Church of Canada was one of the earliest interdenominational church unions of the 20th century. Throughout its existence it has been the largest Protestant church in the country with one in every five Canadians claiming affiliation to it. There have been smaller mergers since, most notably with the Canada Conference of the Evangelical United Brethren.

Changing immigration patterns, the growth of secularism, and rebirth of the religious Right have all served to reduce the United Church's share of the religious mosaic of Canada. As we shall see, there are changes afoot in the land—not the least being that there are now more Muslims in Canada than there are members of the "Continuing" Presbyterian Church.

In Search of the Great Canadian Myth

5: How We Came Out Of It

There is a growing awareness that the world is well into a third wave of transition, the implications of which are destined to be every bit as upsetting as was the Industrial Revolution. The first wave of human transition was from a nomadic to an agricultural way of life; the second was the changeover from agricultural to an industrial society; the third—and the one in which most of the world's developed nations are currently engaged—is the move into a post-industrial age in which information flow, micro-electronics and bio-technology will be the dominant factors. Like everybody else, Canadians are having a great deal of difficulty coping with that Third Wave. One reason why is that the national cultural myths were laid down during the nation's agricultural, First Wave, years.

Like most others raised in industrial second wave society, I was brought up to think of "myths" as being fairy stories—imaginative, but not "true." It's part of the bias of technological humanity that only "facts" are considered to be "true." Less sophisticated societies, on the other hand, are well aware that there are some aspects of reality which are so fundamentally "true" that they can be expressed only in story form. If we are to understand our own unconscious reactions to contemporary events, and our own cultural myopia, then we need to rescue the concept of "myth" from its contemporary Babylonian captivity.

Linguistic philosophers refer to an individual's "blik"—that fixed point of reference by which the individual evaluates every piece of data that comes along. Almost by definition we are unaware of the nature of our personal blik, but that does not make it any less operative in our lives. We need to come to terms with the fact that entire cultures have their "blik," their monomyths—essential plot lines that define what a culture or society believes itself to be.

There are cultures that are very articulate about their myths and tell them frequently—during half-time at football games, at the start of every school day, on civic occasions, whatever.

Other cultures tell their myths subtly. Like Canada's Indians and Inuit (Eskimos) they take their time and spin their stories in a circular motion, letting their legends brood over the deeper meanings.

Then there are cultures that haven't got around to thinking much about their myths and monomyths. Canada, I believe, falls into this latter category.

Cultural Myths

A group of us sat around after class one day last fall: an American pastor, a German theolog, a Kenyan bishop, and a Canadian journalist. We were acknowledging how hard it is to understand what Jesus is saying about the nature of the Kingdom of God in His parables, because of the way in which we all of us *acculturate* the message. We filter the radicalness of Jesus' gospel through our own cultural monomyths. (Even the gospel writers had the same problem.) In an attempt to examine our own cultural myths in the light of the gospel "myth" we set about trying to identify them.

The American was typically open and direct. "Our national monomyth?" he said: *"He who grabs first—gets!* or perhaps, *Ronald Reagan on an MX Missle riding into town with six-guns ablaze to save the honest white folk from the natives."*

The German was equally frank. "Our basic myth?" he mused. "Probably—*Can anything good come from anywhere else?"*

The Kenyan was thoughtful. "I will tell you," he said "what underlies an African approach to life. It is the understanding: *I am, because We are."*

The Canadian didn't know quite what to say. The Dene of Canada's North have a saying, "The land is my mother," but few white Canadians can understand it, much less identify with it.

Then I set about reading Canadian History in preparation for writing this book, and now I think I know what I should have said during that after-class bull session. Canada's foundational monomyth? *Anyone, by hard work and sacrifice, can make it.* Most Canadians, in their heart of hearts, believe that to be true.

Understandably so. Consider that through all Canada's formative years that was exactly how most of the people survived. They felled the trees, ploughed the land, endured the winters and built a better future for their children. A lot of sweat and some basic intelligence and anybody could achieve success. And if things didn't work out in one place, you moved to another.

Most Canadians still believe that anybody, anywhere in the world, can do the same. All they have to do is get off their butts and get to work. Such thinking conveniently ignores the fact that not everybody has the available land, or exploitable resources, or political freedom that Canadians continue to enjoy. Never mind. Monomyths survive in the emotions; they don't necessarily have to pass through the intellect to exercise authority!

One has also to take seriously the fact that Canadians have achieved the "good life" without ever having experienced a revolution. Early French Canadian society was founded on a respect for authority and order. The Loyalists chose deliberately *not* to be part of a revolution and paid a considerable price for it. Consequently, in spite of an instinctive sympathy for the underdogs of this world, Canadians have just an awful time sympathising with revolutionaries. Their reaction would run something like this: "In the first place, if they would talk less and work more they'd build the country they desire; and in the second place, rational people can resolve their differences by talking things out. It takes a bit longer, but it spills a lot less blood."

For instance, in late 1981 Canada's provincial and federal leaders finally came to an agreement on a formula for amending the new Canadian Constitution. They'd been arguing and debating the issue for almost a decade. When they announced the resolution of their differences they said with some pride: "We reached it by consensus, not unilateral action, and that is the Canadian way." Dull maybe, but it really is "the Canadian way!"

Let it be noted, however, that the Quebec francophone nationalists are not yet part of that consensus.

Developing the Myth

We press on, because there is more to the Canadian myth. It's related to the vastness of the country and the sparseness of the population. In Canada you weren't (and aren't) supposed to "grab". It wasn't nice, and you didn't need to. There was plenty there. You and your neighbours were all in this together, all starting pretty well from scratch and it just wasn't necessary or neighbourly to "grab".

Consequently Canadians as a rule aren't terribly pushy people. A bit gauche perhaps, but not really pushy. I remember ending up one time with seven other people on an out-of-the-way corner of the back deck of a Greek island steamer. The French had taken over one lounge, the Americans another, the Swedes had usurped the main deck. There were we seven, off in our little cul-de-sac. We started chatting, and discovered that we were all Canadians!

The French Canadians have added their bit to this side of the Canadian character. If early French Canadians believed in simplicity and hard work they also knew how to have fun. St. Jean Street in Quebec City on a summer evening is like no other city in Canada! The French Canadian may not have as much of the new world's wealth as their Yankee (or even their anglophone Canadian) cousin, but they've probably got fewer ulcers.

So we have to subtly alter that foundation myth. It's not just that by sacrifice and hard work anyone can make it, it's rather—*Anyone, by hard work and sacrifice, can make enough.* Why waste all that energy just to make more?

Though, let it be noted, that what the average Canadian today would consider "enough" would be, by the standards of most of the world's inhabitants, a great deal indeed.

Nor are we quite done yet. There is still another strand running through the Canadian monomyth, and it has to do with the role of government in the lives of Canadians. Maybe it is because of that early opting for law and order, or it may be a remembrance of the brighter side of British paternalism. Whatever its origins, government involvement in the lives and business affairs of the people has never in Canada been the bug-bear which it has been elsewhere.

Without government initiative and assistance the CPR would simply never have been built. The Loyalists would not have survived their first winter without government help. Many of the prairie settlers could not have come to Canada had not the government paid their way. If capitalism is not a dirty word in the Canadian dictionary, neither is socialism. Canadians pay taxes, 20%-50% of their individual earnings, from which their various levels of government then provide community services, health and medical care, education, welfare, unemployment insurance, disability and old age pensions for all. So, if really pressed, the average Canadian would probably have to revise that foundational monomyth just a shade more and admit that in practice, if not in theory, it should read—*Anyone, by hard work and sacrifice, and with a bit of organized cooperation, can make enough.*

It's kind of a nice monomyth to believe in. But it's been getting a heavy working over by developments since. And some Canadians have finally noticed that it has left to one side the experience of one whole segment of the Canadian mosaic—namely the nation's original inhabitants.

Section III

CANADA DURING THE SECOND WAVE

Changes Subtle and Inexorable.

1: The People of the Land

As Canada moved into the years of its industrial revolution it left behind a culture that had existed in the land for over 30,000 years. Native Indian culture was based on such a totally different world-view from that of the predominantly European migration that flooded into the country, that it was impossible to blend the two. Native culture was simply submerged by sheer numbers and superior technology.

I once did a week of radio features in which a native Indian woman told what it is like to grow up Indian in a white society. It was incredibly moving material. Heart-rending. Compelling. I had to spend hours editing the original tape in an attempt both to do justice to Dinah Schooner's story and yet to get it into a format which would fit the white-man's medium.

One of Dinah's chief complaints was that she had grown up knowing all about Capt. Cook and Alexander MacKenzie, Napoleon and Queen Victoria, but nobody knew about her. Nobody knew about Bella Coola Salish. Not even (and most devastatingly) she.

On another occasion I was privileged to be the Church Conference's representative to the 100th Anniversary celebrations of the arrival of the famous missionary, Thomas Crosby, at the northern B.C. coastal native village of Port Simpson. Crosby travelled up and down that awesome coastline by canoe—we went by the church's modern and considerably larger motor vessel which bears his name.

What struck me most about the Anniversary service was the eyes of the Indian kids in the front row. They took in everything that was going on—the choir from the thoroughly Americanized village of their Alaskan cousins from across the strait, the electric guitars and gospel songs of the rock group from the local Pentecostal congregation, the sermon by a former missionary, and the stolid stoicism of their own elders. What their eyes said to me as they took in each of those in turn was: "I don't think I'm that ... that's not me ... I'm not that either ... I don't want to be that ... but then who am I?" The number of teenage suicides in B.C.'s native coastal villages is alarming. And understandable.

A History of Canada's Native Peoples

Archeologists suggest that as early as 40,000 B.C. Cro-Magnon hunters crossed the ice-bridge from Asia to Alaska. Certainly by 8000 B.C. there were independent native cultures flourishing on the Canadian plains and on the British Columbia coast. While the Druids were busily constructing Stonehenge and the Pharoahs their pyramids along the Nile, the first tribes of foraging native Indians were establishing themselves in what is now southern Ontario. At the same time and far to the north, the Inuit were creating their unique Eskimo culture.

North American native cultures were intricate and sophisticated. There was an extensive trading system; fishing, hunting and trapping areas were carefully defined and jealously defended; all-out wars between tribes seldom occurred, more because the economy and social organization of the tribes could not sustain it than because Indians were by nature more peaceable than Europeans.

The whites devastated this ordered civilization. They inflated its money supply with their glass beads, brought death to the majority of the original 280,000 inhabitants with their diseases, and introduced guns, steel, gunpowder, horses and whisky to the art of tribal warfare. The greed of the traders in the European competition for furs soon had the natives involved in the destruction of their own habitat.

There has been some recent research which suggests that there may in fact be *physiological* differences between races in the way their bodies react to alcohol. Be that as it may, *psychologically* alcohol had a horrendous impact on Indian society. Capt. Cook wrote in his diary that when he offered "spirituous liquors" to B.C.'s natives "they rejected them as something unnatural to the palate." This did not long remain the case as traders brought in cheap whisky by the keg for use in bartering for furs. The whisky acted to cut off the controlling influences of custom and taboo and introduced into native society a phenomenon almost unknown up to that point—*intra*-tribal violence.

Thomas Crosby writes of sitting in council with a tribe near Ladysmith on Vancouver Island. A young brave, under the influence of alcohol, had shot his own father. "Oh missionary," one old brave said, "You bring us good words, the Book tells of good things, but look at that dead chief. Are you not ashamed of your white brother? Why don't you convert him? He had the Book. Why doesn't he stop making and selling whisky? Why don't you convert the man who gave the liquor to that man who shot his own father?" Crosby wrote. "As the old orator poured forth his eloquent address in his own language, I felt, for the first time, ashamed that I was a white man."[8]

Some Indian leaders, particularly amongst the Iroquois in the East and the Blackfeet in the West, were very much aware that the growing tide of immigration from Europe was a threat to their land and livelihood. Fifty years before the *Mayflower* sailed and even before Champlain's efforts at colonization in New France the Iroquois had forged a federation to preserve their trade routes and territories. The Hurons and Algonquins opted out and chose instead to get rich by trading furs with the French, thus enabling the European powers to exploit the Indian tribes one against the other.

The Iroquois confederacy was used and then destroyed, first by the British and then by the Americans. Chief Pontiac and his warriors put up a fierce struggle during the Indian Wars of 1763-66, killing more than 2000 settlers and some 500 British troops. But when the British offered to reserve the land beyond the Appalachian Mountains for the Indians, the latter switched over to the British side during the American War of Independence. When the Americans won, many of the Iroquois came to Canada, particularly after their final defeat at Tippecanoe a decade later.

On the Plains and in the North there was relatively little open strife between natives and new settlers—in the far north because so few settlers ventured there and on the plains partly because the missionaries came first.

Native People and the Church

Many of the current native leaders express a lot of anger towards the church. They regard missionaries as the shock troops of European cultural imperialism, robbing them of their spirituality, their heritage and their land. The old gag is repeated: "When the white man came he had the Bible and we had the land. He taught us to pray and when we opened our eyes we had the Bible and he had the land." It always gets a nervous laugh from guilt-ridden whites but it's neither fair nor true. With or without the Bible, with or without the church, Canada's native peoples would have lost their land and their culture. What was going on was conquest pure and simple, however polite the words of the treaty-makers. The presence and influence of the church did keep the bloodshed and the strife to a minimum, but if the Indians had instead chosen to fight it out, they would have been no more successful in Canada than they were in the United States.

It is true though that even Crosby, Bompas and Lacombe were the products of their own age. With the best intentions in the world they could not help but exercise cultural imperialism. Along with most of their fellows they failed to appreciate Indian spirituality and culture. But what they did understand all too clearly was that the way of life that had supported that culture was doomed to extinction. The buffalo on the prairie were exterminated before the end of the century, ancient hunting grounds were traversed by fences, forests were stripped and denuded of game. And the Indians themselves played their part in that destruction.

If the nomadic life-style was doomed, then the only hope for the natives lay in learning the arts of agriculture and industry, and in learning the white man's language and ways, so reasoned some of the church pioneers. They built model agricultural stations and established schools for Indian children. Some of the schools were models of Christian caring; in others, Indian children were strapped for speaking their native language.

Reluctantly the surviving tribes entered into treaties with first the British and then the new Canadian government. (Only a few, like the Nishgas of northern British Columbia, are in the interesting legal position of never having relinquished their land by treaty nor having been officially "conquered".) They retreated to designated reservations which have been, for successive Canadian legislatures, primary targets for the location of roads, bridges, transmission lines, and all the other support systems of urban industrialism.

In the past few decades there have arisen Indian leaders who are no longer content to take what the Department of Indian Affairs is prepared to give them. Mainline churches have, on the whole, been supportive of their efforts. But the outcome of the struggle is far from clear, and the Indians far from unanimous about their own positions.

A Distinctive Culture

Native Canadian culture knew a great deal about being an individual-in-community, about (w)holistic ways of thinking, and about spirituality. Some native cultures were feudal and hierarchical, others were run by group consensus, still others were essentially matrilineal, but in all of them the individual existed as part of a people.

One of the earliest chroniclers of Indian life in Canada recorded his astonishment at the sophistication of the communal life amongst the Iroquois. He wrote: "They have such absolute notions of liberty that they allow no kind of superiority of one over another, and banish all servitude from their territories. There is not a man in the magistracy of the Five Nations who has gained his office otherwise than by merit. Their authority is only the esteem of the people, and ceases the moment that esteem is lost."[9] In Indian society, no one was forced to act upon the orders of someone whose judgment he or she mistrusted.

Children in a native village were, and still are, loved and raised by dozens of aunts and uncles (a fact not yet grasped by provincial welfare authorities who are too quick, in Indian eyes, to remove children from parental homes deemed unsuitable by the department). Children were and are seldom sharply reprimanded or punished, which helps to explain the deep resentment amongst adult Indians over the style of discipline meted out in some residential schools. Even with adults the chief instrument of community control was simply public ridicule.

The product of all this upbringing tended to be, in an earlier age, a supremely self-confident, ego-centred, self-willed adult who would not lightly accept—*or offer*—reprimands or orders, contradictions or punishment. The other side of the coin was a complex system of precepts, customs and taboos which held the community together as a unit.

Most of this was so foreign to the mindset of European settlers, including the missionaries, that it sailed clean over their heads.

Sexuality

The Europeans were equally nonplussed by the Indian approach to human sexuality. Prostitution was unknown amongst the Indians. The chiefs were at first puzzled and then delighted that fur traders wanted to pay for a woman—whether for a night or for a more permanent arrangement. To the Indians sexual gratification was both normal and healthy. Polygamy was the norm in most tribes (how else were surplus women to survive?) and a good hunter would often marry several sisters. Wives could be freely loaned to tribal brothers, even to strangers, and were at perfect liberty to enjoy the experience. Any resultant children were no problem since they belonged to the whole tribe anyway.

In Iroquois culture the women owned not only the children but all the tribal property and equipment. Divorce was simple, the woman simply put the man's few possessions outside her tepee and he went back to live with his mother and sisters. There was no disgrace attached to such an occurrence, for why should two people live together if they were unhappy? Similarly, pre-marital sex was encouraged. Why marry and find out that you were incompatible?

To the European steeped in "Christian" morality with its emphasis on chastity, monogamy, abstention from "animal" pleasures, and notions of romantic love, all of this seemed nothing but debased and pagan promiscuity.

The whites were similarly disinclined to respect native spirituality. Native religion really didn't separate people and other earth-creatures. Animals were regarded as persons, in some aspects of their existence possessing superior skills to human beings (e.g: ability to fly). Christian monotheism could not comprehend the spiritual sensitivity of those who sought to honour the spirit of God in the forest, or the raven, or the whale; many a fiery missionary sermon was preached against the "Baal gods" of the new world!

The B.C. Indians, for instance, had an important element in their social/religious life called the Potlatch. The missionaries saw it as debauchery and tried to stamp it out. The Potlatch was a grand and glorious party, and after the traders' arrival it did often include more alcohol than was good for it. But its original intention was a sort of biblical Year of Jubilee. A tribal member who had been materially blessed was expected to give a feast and provide gifts for everybody in the village. The gift-giving incurred a debt of repayment on the part of the recipient and thus the village's capital was kept in circulation. Not at all a bad system of social welfare.

Every tribe and village had its shaman and much of what was done in the name of religion was superstition. But underneath there was a (w)holistic approach to creation and an awareness of the transcendent realities of the universe. Even those early Jesuits at Huronia had an appreciation of the way in which the Hurons valued their dreams and other "right-brain" experiences and tried to relate the Christian experience of God to it.

A Shocking Culture

The Indians were shocked by a culture in which some could have plenty and others go hungry. In the tribal village everything was shared, even with the friendly stranger. Many a Canadian settler survived the first years because an Indian would appear at his door with a gift of food. The Indians taught the whites how to plant corn and beans, how to make dishes from birch bark, clothing and bedding from hides, even how to catch fish and survive on wild roots, nuts and herbs.

Canada's Indians selflessly, and in keeping with their culture, helped the white man to settle in the country. But the whites saw their tribal sexuality as promiscuity, their lack of materialistic ambition as laziness, their unconcern over detail as unreliability, their ultimate struggle to protect their homeland as savagery, and their unfortunate intolerance of alcohol as a sign of inferiority. If they could not be assimilated, then for their own and everybody else's sake, they must be placed on reserves. When they wandered off and ran afoul of the white man's law they should be put in jail, which is where an inordinately high percentage of Indians in Canada are today.

It is not a pretty picture, but Canada's Indians, in their basic mindset and approach to God and the created order, may be much more capable of surviving Canada's Third Wave than they were of its Second; perhaps more capable than their fellow Canadians who are bogged down in the sterility of a linear, consumer-oriented world of "facts and things."

Duke Redbird, one of Canada's prominent native leaders, has remarked that the Indians have already waited 300 years for the white man to catch up, and are prepared to wait a few more.

2: Canada's Churches—
Custodians of the Myth

Meanwhile, "back on the ranch," the rest of Canada was getting on with its transition to a predominantly Second Wave culture. And if there were elements of racism in its treatment of its native people, they at least had the small comfort of knowing that they were not alone! One of the earliest assaults on the Canadian myth of neighbourliness came in British Columbia (BC). From the start this province had a polyglot population and its location on the Pacific rim meant that many of them were oriental. In the early days of the gold rush there had been isolated racial incidents. Then the CPR brought in boatloads of Chinese labourers to work on the construction of the transcontinental railroad. Many of them stayed on. In fact in 1910 the B.C. population included 21 different nationalities worshipping 47 different versions of the Almighty!

Some B.C. people, including influential church members, decided that "neighbourliness" had gone far enough. They formed the Asiatic Exclusion League to put a lid on oriental immigration. As the depression of 1906 deepened the populace's need for a scapegoat grew. The Asiatics made a visible target and in 1907 there were race riots in the streets of Vancouver. Events came to a head in 1914 when an entire shipload of Sikh labourers were refused permission to land in Vancouver harbour. After nine weeks of bitter litigation the *Komogata Maru* and its starving passengers were sent back to sea.

It was a foretaste of things to come. During the Second World War Canada joined the U.S. in evacuating its entire Japanese population from the coastal areas. Some of those sent to the hastily constructed resettlement camps in the Interior were second and even third-generation Canadians. Their fishing boats and homes on the Lower Mainland were confiscated and sold at ridiculous prices. Sgt. Buck Suzuki was the man who gave the surrender order to the Japanese forces at the end of the war. Though he had spent the entire war fighting for the Canadian army in the jungles of Southeast Asia, he came home to find that his house, lot and furniture—valued by the tax assessor at $7,000—had been sold at auction for less than $2,000, his wife and children having long since been forcibly removed to Ontario.

There were some in the churches who, almost alone, stood by the Japanese during those bitter years. On my first pastorate, deep in the mountain valleys of the BC Interior, were the remains of some of those camps to which the Japanese had been evacuated. A few of the Japanese were still there and we sipped tea together in their little "House of Glad Tidings" and reminisced about the women workers of the Women's Missionary Society who had come to them in those years and created schools for their children. One old church elder remarked: "I saw that the church, only the Christian church, was a friend to us. It must have been hard for them to be friends with the enemy people but they helped us. They were people of God much more than they were Canadians. That's why I became a Christian and I am today proud of being a Christian."[10]

World War I

It wasn't just racism that was shattering the Canadian myth. The whole veneer of genteel "Christian civilization" was under assault. The carnage of World War I was evidence enough that the world was changing—and not necessarily for the better.

At the start of that conflict only a very few church leaders presumed to question its legitimacy. The majority of church people went dutifully to war for God, King and Country. Some churches served as army recruiting depots, the Ladies Aid knitted socks for the boys at the front, and those clergy not at the front had their hands full ministering to the bereaved at home.

In French Canada the issues were not nearly so clear. The Boer War had aroused mixed feelings in Quebec where public sentiment ran strongly in favour of the Boers (who were, after all, another minority being "oppressed" by the British). Francophone Canadians enlisted readily enough in defence of France and Belgium at the start of World War I but by the time conscription was instituted in 1917, defections started to become evident. Fighting for Canada was one thing. Fighting to save the British was something else again.

Industrialism and Church Responses

Canada went into World War I an agricultural nation. It emerged an industrialized nation. It was only a matter of time before myth and reality would clash. They met head on in 1919 in the Winnipeg General Strike.

There had been minor strikes before in Canada but nothing to equal this one. Its causes were obvious enough. Demobilized soldiers, returning home to a hero's welcome, soon found that there was no place for them in the nation's work force. Added to their number were thousands of wartime workers whose jobs had disappeared almost literally before the ink on the peace treaties was dry.

More than 33,000 Winnipeg workers took to the barricades. For a time the Strike Committee was the de facto government of the city. Then the violence escalated. Royal Canadian Mounted Police (RCMP), reinforced by special strike police, charged the picket lines and the blood flowed. The churches for the most part were caught flat-footed. There were those like Canon F. G. Scott (senior chaplain of the Canadian Forces) who came to appeal on behalf of his "boys." Some of the church academics and theological professors pitched in on the side of the strikers. But for the most part the church leadership had little to contribute.

One significant exception was J. S. Woodsworth, a Methodist clergyman and son of the Methodist Superintendent of Missions. Woodsworth played a major role in mediating the strike but he did not stop there. Unlike Papineau and Mackenzie, Woodsworth was an organizer as well as an orator. He set about building and organizing what was to become one of Canada's three major political parties, the CCF (Canadian Commonwealth Federation), now known as the New Democratic Party. The party was built on social democratic principles. It has had many well-known Canadian clergy in its ranks and several times at its head. One result has been that socialism in Canada has had a much more humanitarian (and less Marxist) face than have labour/socialist movements in some other parts of the world. Woodsworth found that not all of his church colleagues were sympathetic to his cause and he finally resigned from the ministry, thought he continued to lead a Bible class in his home congregation for many years.

Woodsworth and others forced the Canadian churches to face the fact that there is an inherent dichotomy between being keepers of the cultural myth and being prophets of social justice. Priest and prophet have never existed comfortably together, particularly in times of rapid and fundamental structural change. At such times people look to the church to reaffirm traditional values and meanings. For the church it means the almost impossible task of trying to be both glue and yeast at the same time!

Most of the mainline churches realized that they had to evolve some sort of new social philosophy. Even a social gospel predicated on the inevitable march of humanity towards progress seemed in doubt. Previously, social problems had been dealt with by having another revival and recalling individuals to a more rigorous personal morality. As valid as that was, it seemed somehow inadequate to meet the challenge of the forces at work behind the events of the Strike (not to mention the War).

Initially the Roman Catholics did a better job than the Protestants of dealing with the realities of the industrial revolution. They set up training schools for co-operatives and created a labour movement of their own which as early as 1911 had over 350,000 members. The mainline Protestants ended up mouthing most of the right words but none of them ever became truly "blue collar" churches. Nor were any of them really able to come to terms with the power struggles between massified capital and big organized labour which are inherent in industrialism.

Depression and Revival

But the churches weren't alone in that. Even some of the people involved didn't understand what was happening and before any of them could get it all figured out the world was plunged into a global depression followed by a global war. After the war came an era of growth and prosperity that lulled everybody into believing that the myths were still working. It wasn't until the '60 s that the lid on the pressure cooker started to work loose!

The Great Depression lasted for ten years, from 1929 till the start of the Second World War. It was a dreadful time for Canada. Unemployed men rode the rails, back and forth across the country, looking for work. The nation had no legislation for dealing with an economic catastrophe of such magnitude and so it fell to the volunteer agencies to give assistance. In British Columbia Andrew Roddan at First United Church, Vancouver, became the champion of the down-and-out. He took on City Hall and cajoled supplies from businessmen to keep his soup lines going. There were others like him in cities across the nation. Relief trains were sent from the East to aid prairie farmers hit by the worst drought of the century. And right across the land church manses became known as the contact points for homeless men on the move.

It was a particularly difficult time for the new United Church of Canada. It had come into Union with a surfeit of clergy and now there were just not enough pulpits to go around. My father was one such. Just months before I was born the pulp mill in the town where he was pastoring shut down. Everybody in town—including him—found themselves out of a job.

It was not surprising that sectarian revivalism should reappear at such a time. When people feel powerless, whether because of economic uncertainty, government oppression, impossible global problems, or insuperable personal ones, that is the time when revival occurs. The deeper the despair, the more charismatic, apocalyptic and biblically authoritarian the revival.

Pentecostalism had evolved world-wide during the first decade of the 20th century, although Canada's 1911 census showed only 515 Pentecostals in the entire nation. However by 1951 there were more than 95,000.

In Alberta fundamentalist faith and conservative politics came together to form a new political party, Social Credit. William Aberhart might have remained an unknown local preacher had it not been for his exploitation of the new medium, radio. His weekly "Back to the Bible" radio broadcasts expanded into a Bible college. To his dogma of biblical inerrancy he added Major Douglas' economic theories with such success that in 1935 he was swept into power as premier of the province.

Alberta has remained staunchly conservative ever since, and is now home to several thriving fundamentalist Bible schools. All of them preach a non-denominational form of Christian unity based on a commitment to the literal interpretation of Scripture (rather than on commitment to doctrine or a form of church government). With the return of the "good times" after the war, Pentecostalism leveled off in Canada. It is significant, and not surprising, that it is once again on the increase.

War and Reconstruction

The Second World War found Canada better prepared than it had been for the First. Rationing, veterans' benefits, baby bonuses, and family allowances all helped to prevent a repetition of the Winnipeg strike. There was more readiness in the churches to question the whole idea of modern warfare and more than one RCMP agent spent part of the war years in church, taking notes on sermons preached by suspect clerics! But for most Canadians it was the kind of war in which you thought you could still tell the "good guys" from the "bad." It would take Vietnam to disillusion us on that score, and some of us not even then.

The years after the War were a second great boom period for Canada. A new influx of European immigrants (Displaced Persons we called them) brought needed skills and energies. The economy expanded. In politics Canada was up to its neck in the United Nations and proud of it. Church attendance soared. The war-baby boom was bursting the Sunday Schools at their seams. Church Extension was everywhere, with a new church, hall or manse going up almost every day.

Ecumenical cooperation was in vogue. The World Council of Churches had been formed, as had the Canadian Council of Churches. The authors of books on the Canadian church were predicting continued growth and an ever -increasing commitment to social justice issues. The Fourth Faith and Order Conference of the WCC met in Montreal and was addressed by Cardinal Leger. The International Anglican Congress met in Toronto later that same year (1963) and the Anglican Church in Canada surged to the forefront of social discourse in the nation. Pierre Berton was commissioned to write *The Comfortable Pew* and the Primate's World Mission Fund was oversubscribed. The great "development decade" and the "green revolution" were going to remedy global imbalances. The church, with spinnaker set and sails wing on wing, was running hard before the wind.

And then, subtly, the winds began to shift.

Beware of Smiling Dragons

3: The Nature of Industrialized Society

To understand that shift in the wind requires a look at the nature of industrialism and the social structures which it creates.

In Canada, the post-war years were so good, for so many, that people began to believe life could and should go on that way indefinitely. They even gave with considerable generosity to help the rest of the world "catch up." Had they looked more deeply into their own infrastructures, they might have seen what those structures were doing to others and to themselves.

The New Testament writers were not unaware of the impact upon human life of the "principalities and powers" of this world. It was their way of acknowledging (among other things) that there are powerful social, political and economic forces which shape the way in which humans relate to their world and to each other.

Western liberal thought has never been very comfortable with such analyses of the human condition. It prefers rather to believe in individual human thought and initiative as an adequate catalyst of social change. Karl Marx, for his part, made no bones about economic determinism. For him it was the engine that drives human history inexorably onwards and upwards towards the socialist utopia.

More recently, however, some Western sociologists (e.g: Peter Berger), while rejecting theories of rigid determinism, have been making the case that *Industrialism does have within it an intrinsic set of relationships, mindsets, and socio-economic infrastructures.* In other words, once a society has decided to worship at the shrine of industrialization, other fundamental decisions about the future shape of that society have, in that act, unconsciously also been made. Subsequently one can fine-tune the structures, make them less or more humane, but from there on, if you want the benefits of industrialism, you have to play by its rules.

Bad news as this is for Western liberals, it is worse news for those in the developing world who hope to industrialize (so as to cash in on the "good life") and yet retain their traditional culture. The first objective has become improbable and the second impossible. After spending considerable time in every one of the world's major industrialized nations Alvin Toffler concludes that regardless of whether the nation is run by state capitalism or private capitalism, is in the Orient or in Europe, in the Northern hemisphere or the Southern, certain common and fundamental features of industrialized society eventually predominate.

It is possible to miss this fact because the surface expressions of those underlying similarities may look so different. It requires some reflection, for instance, to see that the Hell's Angels, the Moonies, and the Red Guards have a lot in common. But all are expressions of the same basic need, the individual's need to belong to a group. And that need is a fundamental feature of urbanization and its accompanying sense of cultural anomie. Failure to acknowledge this common rootage can lead to a lot of wasted effort arguing the relative merits of the differing fruits at the ends of the branches.

Industrialized nations that delight in "putting down" American culture might want to think seriously about the probability that they would have evolved something very similar, were not American models so readily available—to use, copy and criticize!

We need to examine carefully what is optional and *extrinsic*, and what is fundamental and *intrinsic* to living with industrialism. This distinction has to do not so much with *what* people think about, as *how* they think about it. For instance, jet engine manuals tend to be written in English but the *language* is really *extrinsic;* the manuals could as easily be written in Swahili. The engineering *mentality* however is *intrinsic*.

I watched a group of construction workers in Zambia spend half an hour attempting to start the motor on a gasoline-powered cement mixer. They were marvellously cheerful about the whole affair (I would have been cursing the beast in a blind rage after the first five minutes). They took turns, one after an other, patiently winding and yanking on that blessed starter cord. For all I know they are at it yet. But what they really needed was not just a willingness to work. What they needed was somebody like my next-door neighbour who *thinks* like a gasoline engine! *That's* what *intrinsic* means.

Building Infrastructures

Intrinsic to industrialism are a whole set of infrastructures which, if they are not there, have to be built. And which if they are not then built, leave a void of endless frustrations.

I recall friends in Trinidad expressing their frustration over this basic lack of infrastructure, even in that relatively affluent part of the developing world. It's a common complaint. Bureaucracies that don't function, phones that don't work, roads that are in disrepair, grandiose development schemes that fail to deliver.

I visited some church-sponsored chicken farms in an African state. They were going broke because of a lack of chicken feed. There was feed all right—500 miles away in the capital city. But nobody in the government bureaucracy had been able to work out a plan for transporting it to the farmers.

Many a third world nation functioned within the industrial world (albeit mainly as a producer of primary resources) while it was an appendage within the colonial ruler's total infrastructure. But when independence came, the structures disappeared with the departing colonial administrators and bankers. And unfortunately, having primary resources and a determination to build a better world for your children just isn't a big enough "leg-up" to get you into the industrial sweepstakes at this point in history.

The options for developing nations today are not all that attractive. If they want to have industrialism and lack either the time, the space, or the resources to *grow* the necessary industrial infrastructures by consensus and experimentation, then they face having the structures *imposed*—either from the Right (as in Korea and the Philippines) or from the Left (as in Afghanistan and Ethiopia). Small wonder so many third world nations are asking if there is not some other way to arrange for the production and distribution of the Earth's resources.

Canada was lucky. It inherited much of its economic infrastructure ready-made from Great Britain. This provided some initial capital and the country possessed the land, the resources and the time to develop more. But it is interesting to note that even the other European powers, bogged down as they were even into the 19th century by the Napoleonic Wars, had a difficult time breaking into the industrialized club. The Austrian marginalist economists of that day leveled the same complaints against British laissez-faire monetary policies which contemporary third world proponents of a New International Economic Order level at the West: "Fine for you; you're already in. But if we play by your rules, we'll never get in!"

The Nature of the Beast

But once in, and past the dragon's smile, one soon discovers the hard realities of the beast—and those who get the most out of the system are those who design infrastructures that cater to those realities.

Concentration. In feudal societies one village market didn't need to worry much about what was going on in the next. Industrialized societies, however, require large concentrations of capital and production facilities. These factors bring about a concentration of population (everywhere that industrialization goes, rural populations decline and urban populations explode). The very abundance of goods produced requires a concentration of markets to facilitate their exchange.

Centralization. As the stakes get bigger, the centres of decision-making become fewer and need more often to seek each other out. Greater demands upon the infrastructure require a bigger role for government, so political power starts to centralize. And since industrialized societies consume vast amounts of energy, particularly fossil fuels, these too come to require centralized organization and control.

Standardization. The industrialized world is a "mass synchronized society." Canadians may or may not want to be proud of the fact that it was Sandford Fleming, the Canadian who surveyed the route for the Canadian Pacific Railroad, who designed those global time zones which keep the whole world dutifully marching to the beat of Greenwich Mean Time! In a complex and inter-related world, products, systems and procedures need to interact in similar and predictable ways. It takes a lot of the spice and variety out of life but at least a "Big Mac" is always a "Big Mac"—whether in Brussels, Bangkok, or Boston.

In all of the industrialized societies education has become an important adjunct of the production process. Industrial society needs few philosophers but many technicians. It requires citizens who will be punctual, obedient, and conditioned to doing repetitive work. It's very hard to run a competitive business if the workers only show up when they feel like it! Better they should learn in school to arrive on time and produce on schedule.

Consistency. Peter Berger points out that the natural sciences are foundational to the industrial system, and that they are very much dependent upon the world behaving in a consistent and predictable manner (two parts hydrogen, one part oxygen, one electrical spark and the result had better be water every time). Similarly technology, that offspring of the natural sciences, also requires predictable and consistent performance (the microchips in the computer on which I am writing this book had better behave the same way each time I push a certain key or I'm in big trouble!). Berger goes on to suggest that ultimately industrial society requires the same kind of predictability from its human components, each of us dutifully conforming to the categories assigned to us by the bureaucracy.

Bureaucracy and technocracy love each other, for both of them regard the Universe as one vast "filing cabinet in the sky!"

Massification. It's the bottom line for industrialized civilization. "Small is Beautiful" is a foreign concept to a system which depends for its functioning on a maximization of profits, production and consumption at the limits of their marginal utility. "If one hardware store is good, two must be better" runs the logic of massification. So the system compounds itself. Big businesses gobble little businesses; big unions form to conteract big business; big government is created to both service and control the activities of the unions and the businesses; big profits lead to big investments abroad requiring big armies to protect the investments; and all of it bulwarked by big education at home!

Undergirding the entire enterprise is mass communication. Large integrated systems require the support of large numbers of people, so the control of information flow becomes a priority concern. It is not by chance that every political revolutionary in the world, whether a general or a wild-eyed radical, heads first for control of the national media.

4: What Industrialism Does To People

This then is the nature of industrialized society. For the church the critical question then becomes, "What does all this do to *people*?"

On the plus side it has to be acknowledged that industrialism has provided most Canadians with a standard of living which kings and emperors of yore could but dream of. But there are some less attractive side effects.

Industrialization has affected our basic ways of thinking and perceiving. Some fascinating research has been done in the past few decades into the functioning of the human brain. It now appears evident that each of us has two "brains," the left hemisphere and the right. They are of course interconnected but they function in quite different though complementary ways. The left hemisphere programmes information in linear and sequential fashion (like a computer), whereas the right hemisphere thinks and perceives in patterns and wholes. The left controls most of our mechanical functions, the right processes our emotional reactions. One of the major frustrations of poets, painters and mystics down through the ages has been the necessity and difficulty of communicating their profoundly right-brain experiences through left-brain channels—their own and others.

Of critical importance is the fact that the brain hemisphere which senses it can best deal with any given situation is the one which cuts in and takes over the individual's responses. Industrial society is very much wedded to left-brain processes. Its educational system is predicated on them (which may explain why Einstein was a failure in school). Consequently its citizens tend to react instinctively, and often inappropriately, with left-brain responses.

Westerners function very well as pragmatists and doers. Nobody can run a production line better. But they are paying a fearful price for downgrading the (w)holistic, emotional and spiritual side of their being. Not enough of them know how to question whether the production line should be there at all.

Recently I did some biblical studies on the parables of Jesus. Like most in my culture I had first learned the parables in Sunday School where they were held up as example stories for good Christians to emulate. I had to unlearn most of that and rediscover my imagination before I could hear the music of parable song and risk its invitation to the dance. I recall our professor coming back almost in despair from leading a three-day extension course with some parish clergy. "Facts and actions!" he expostulated. "That's all we seem to understand any more in the church!" (And in the process we have driven most of the poets and intellectuals out).

If some Western Christians are running off after charismatic renewal it may well be because Western Christianity has been starving their right-brains and with it their souls. Fellowship groups and folkmasses may feed the human need for community. They do not well supply the soul's need to experience transcendence.

The culture of Canada's native peoples has always been much more intrinsically spiritual and (w)holistic (more right-brain) than that of the Europeans who came and settled in the land. Which helps to explain why non-native Canadians have never been able to fully understand the Indians, and why Canada's Indians have never really been able to "adapt" to the ways of the whites.

In the best of all possible worlds a human being is valued for what he or she *is* (i.e. a child of God). Within the world of the so-called "Protestant work ethic" a person tends to be valued for what she can *produce*. It is ironic that one consequence of working at that ethic has been the creation of a society in which persons are measured by what they *consume!*

Industrial Society Affects Our Value Systems

The value we place on each other is also affected by industrial society. In simpler societies one's relationships tended to be few and profound. In a complex urban environment one interacts with a great many people in the course of a day, but only functionally and in relation to isolated portions of one's existence. To survive, one has to make *oneself* the centre of that complex of connections and keep others at a proper distance.

Marx described the alienation which industrialism brings

to the work place (an alienation between workers and their means of production). But the alienation runs deeper than that. Sociologists have discovered that the more work and life get separated from each other, the easier it becomes to distance other aspects of one's existence. People start to regard what they *do* and the *roles* they fulfill in society, as being something other than what they *are*. So it becomes possible for Christians to pray one thing and live another.

Ultimately the social system itself becomes the victim of the schizophrenia of its members. There no longer seems anything wrong with "ripping-off" the system since one has ceased to acknowledge any ownership of it. When Grant Maxwell did his major study of Canadian attitudes for the Canadian Conference of Catholic Bishops[11] he found a universal distrust of big institutions, no matter what kind, including the church. He also discovered what he came to describe as "an epidemic of loneliness" amongst Canadians in every walk of life.

Industrial society has raised our GNP, but it is now exacting its pound of human flesh in payment.

Industrialism Challenges the Traditional Role of Religion

Not that long ago, in any town or city of the predominantly Christianized parts of the world, a church spire would be the dominant symbol on the horizon. But the church has ceased to be the focal point of the community; the modern city has replaced it with the bank tower.

Given the major role which religion has played in the development of Canada, it sounds incongruous for a Canadian Christian to argue that the church should stay out of politics. "Look," one of them said to me recently, "I have my political party for doing that, just as I have my business for earning a living, my racquet club for physical conditioning, my home for my family life, and my church for my spiritual life."

That kind of compartmentalizing of life would be very foreign to the people who wrote the Bible but it is entirely consistent with the industrial mind-set. Religion is no longer seen to be the keystone which holds the social edifice together.

Rather it is regarded as one department within that edifice. Or as one wit put it recently: "Religion is what consenting adults do in the privacy of their sanctuary."

Religion has become a consumer commodity. One picks from the available market a brand which suits one's individual needs.

5: How We Came Out of It

Such then are the forces at play in Second Wave society. It remains to examine how they are affecting Canadian institutions, and in particular the church.

After more than 15 years in commercial broadcasting I have come, reluctantly, to the conclusion that like the other structures of second wave society it too enslaves those who work in it. Maybe it's the constant deadlines, the seductiveness of power, or maybe just the need to compete for an even bigger slice of the market with the accompanying requirement to "entertain" the audience. But when you end up having to condense complex issues of human existence into 40-second news clips, you end up stereotyping life into categories which it it *not*. And since information media are such an integral part of industrialized society, the reinforcing of preconceived stereotypes just goes on and on.

One of the current stereotypes in Canadian media has to do with the state of organized religion in the country. Recently I watched a TV exposé of one of the new TV evangelists. It was prefaced by the announcer's authoritative voice telling us that *traditional* Christianity is dead in Canada. The pictures on the screen were those which the camera crew could shoot within easy driving distance of the downtown studios: inner city 'cathedrals' with a sprinkling of elderly parishioners, pictures of once grand city churches now sold to the Hare Krishnas, others boarded up and awaiting the wrecker.

What doesn't get reported, because it doesn't fit the stereotype, is the population shift to the suburbs. Many suburban churches are bursting at the seams.

There is however an element of truth in the stereotype. Church membership statistics for virtually all of Canada's mainline churches did decline through the 1970s. Bruce McLeod, then moderator of the United Church, was fond of saying, "We're not dying, we're dieting!" With the fat trimmed away you knew that what was left was solid quality. He may have been right. The decline has leveled off in many mainline denominations and in some, membership and attendance have actually inched upwards again.

On the surface Canada seems still to be a very religious and seemingly Christian nation. The latest census figures show that 90% of Canadians identify with some religious group and three-fourths of them consistently list their affiliation as being with one of the "big three": The Roman Catholic, United or Anglican churches.

Signs of Change

However two recent studies[12] into the nature of religious commitment in Canada make it clear that whatever people tell the census taker, some profound changes have occurred within the last 30 years since the post-War religion boom.

Secularism, that by-product of industrialism, has made serious inroads into the Canadian religious ethos. I grew up in a small town in northern Quebec. The anglophone community was fairly small and there was only the one Protestant church. All the kids I went to school with and played with went to Sunday School, Cubs, Mission Band, etc., at the church. But my own son, growing up in suburban Vancouver, finds that he is the only one of his chums who relates to the congregation of which we are a part (and furthermore he doesn't like Sunday School).

The studies indicate that church involvement has dropped

by fully one-half since the 1950s. Whereas in 1950 *two* of every three Canadians were going to church on some kind of a regular basis and taking (or sending) their children to Sunday School, in 1980 only *one* in every three is doing so. Many of those no longer going to church are the ones who were bursting the seams of Canada's Sunday Schools during the '50s and '60s.

The Growth of Secularism

Reg Bibby, a Canadian sociologist specializing in the study of religion, has concluded that the net impact of higher education, scientific advance and technological innovation has been to turn Canadians earthward. People are seeking answers to life's questions elsewhere than in religion. "A technological fix for every problem" seems to make more sense than belief in a God one cannot see and whose existence cannot be proved. In short, the "God of the Gaps" is starting to feel the pressures of unemployment. There just aren't enough meaningful gaps left.

It will be interesting to see if Canada's 1981 census bears out the findings of these latest studies, but already in the 1971 census there were indications that Bibby's conclusions are probably correct. In every census prior to 1971, fewer than one percent of Canadians identified themselves as having "no religion." In the '71 statistics the No Religion category vaulted into fourth place, right behind the "big three." Over four percent of Canadians placed themselves there and there is every reason to expect the '81 figures to be higher. Secularism is rapidly becoming a way of life for many Canadians—particularly in the West where 13% of B.C.ers said "no religion" to the '71 census taker.

The demographics of this category are significant too. Most of them are young, urban, highly educated, and highly paid. It is the affluent urban younger Canadians who also are having fewer children—in some cases, by deliberate choice, no children at all. Margaret Mead told us that a nation short on children would be short of "future think." Which could explain why many Canadians are content to live with their heads in the sand.

Urbanization's propensity to turn us in on ourselves has also affected the generosity of Canadians. Ten years ago 75% of Canadians on their Income Tax returns claimed the standard $100 deduction for charitable donations. (The standard deduction requires no supporting receipts. You can claim it even if you've given nothing to anyone; but to claim more than the $100 you have to send in receipts.) Last year more than 90% claimed the standard deduction. In other words, in affluent Canada, fewer than 10% of the people are giving more than $100 a year to charities of *any* kind. Either that or a lot of people are losing their receipts.

One could get very discouraged about such statistics if it weren't for the occasional indication that the instinct for caring is still alive. When Terry Fox, a young Canadian who had lost a leg to cancer, set out to *run* across the nation from Newfoundland to his BC home, he captured the imaginations and hearts of all Canadians. Terry made it half-way. When he got to northern Ontario the cancer caught up with him again and made a last and fatal assault upon his body. Terry's funeral was literally a state occasion. And Canadians poured more than $22 million into the Cancer Research Fund in response to his courage and determination. The instinct is still there. Not dead, just disillusioned.

The '60s Life-Style Revolution

If Canada had been less affluent or less politically stable, industrialism's assault on the nation's first wave mythology might first have evidenced itself in the economic or political spheres. As it turned out, it was in the realm of personal life-styles that the crunch first came.

Behind the "hippie" phenomenon of the 1960s was a search for some authority to replace those displaced by modernity. On the premise that any identity is better than none, people flocked to a succession of gurus and tried a kaleidoscope of "trips"—some of them chemically induced. But the ultimate conclusion was that the only relevant authority had to be discovered within the self. "I'm doing my own thing, man" was an incredible threat to parents brought up not to question fundamental values.

Self-discovery groups were a dime-a-dozen. TM, TA, EST .... you could take your pick! For many people (myself included) it was a time of marvellous self-discovery and an introduction to the vast spiritual potential of existentialism. We didn't realize it at the time but part of what was happening was that we were giving our right-brain hemispheres a chance to get in on the action. Congregation members came back from Encounter Weekends and Group Dynamics labs and tried to introduce experiential learning into the worship and group life of the home church. The more traditional members would go home shaking their heads about "all this touchy-feely stuff."

Women's liberation came into its own too. It wasn't new in Canada or in the church. Out of the Temperance Movement of a previous era came the women's suffrage movement led by such colourful and formidable Canadian church women as Nellie McClung. As early as 1936 (early by some yardsticks, 19 centuries late by others) the United Church had ordained women clergy. The leadership of this new struggle for women's rights was not primarily within the church, though the church has remained one of the principal forums for the pursuit of feminist concerns in Canada.

Since the '60s the number of women enrolled in Canada's theological colleges has increased dramatically. Women now comprise one-third of the student body in many Canadian seminaries. But getting jobs in the church after ordination is proving to be something else again. A few "major" congregations have women associate pastors but very few, if any, have a woman as the "senior" minister. There is also a very real backlash. Groups like "Women Aglow" flourish not only in fundamentalist churches.

Gay liberation was not far off the heels of women's liberation. It has yet to become a big issue in the Canadian church but whenever one of Canada's major denominations touches even the fringe of that debate it creates headlines in the media and a furore in many congregations.

The Quiet Revolution in Quebec

The changes effected by industrialization came earlier and

were much more far-reaching in Quebec than any place else in Canada and there they found a political and economic expression. During the 1950's Quebecers began to challenge the traditional values and authority of the Roman Catholic Church. Many of the key figures of contemporary Canadian politics were deeply involved in that movement (Trudeau, Levesque, Chretien, Marchand).

When it was all over, the face of French Canada had been radically altered. A separatist political party was in power with a mandate to preserve French culture and status by taking Quebec out of Confederation if need be. The Roman Catholic Church ceased to be a political power in Quebec. A Franciscan priest, looking back, describes what happened: "Quebec used to have a very organized, traditional Christian culture. Everything was permeated by Catholicism—economics, politics, family life. Religion was omnipresent. All of a sudden Quebec went from a closed society to an open society, from a rural culture to an urban society, from a classical and confessional educational system to a technical and secularist system. In the face of this, what seemed a deep religion was revealed as only a cultural religion."[13]

Another Quebec priest put it this way: "We were brought up to believe that our knowledge was absolute, an exact picture of reality. Our teachers forgot to tell us that the lens was coloured and the camera very narrowly focused."[14]

For one brought up in Quebec it is startling to go back and see the sprawling campuses of the junior colleges and technical schools, while the old convents and residential schools have fallen into disuse and disrepair. But Quebec too is having to face the mixed blessings of industrialism: once you've got the young people off the farms, how do you find jobs for all of them? Still, as one Quebec bishop observed, "The Quiet Revolution in Quebec secularized our institutions without shooting any of our clergy and that is very significant."[15]

The Anomie Remains

If the central theological problem for the early church was *death,* for the Reformation *guilt,* and for the social gospel the problem of *evil,* then surely for industrialized humanity the central theological quest is for *meaning.*

The changes in personal life-style wrought by the '60s continue to be much with us in Canada. Young people living together before marriage (or without it) is commonplace, people are still "doing their own thing," liberation movements continue to work away, marijuana use is down but alcohol consumption is up. Yet under it all, the old sense of *anomie* remains, that gnawing sense that maybe none of it matters anyway.

A middle-aged homemaker says: "Life to me is confusing. Everything contradicts itself. At my age I don't know where I'm going or where my kids are going. I can't really offer them any values any more because you can't be right about anything nowadays. If you didn't laugh, you'd cry, eh?" A civic leader comments: "Religion was a real thing 25 years ago. You had a vision then: marry, have children, be a success, go to church." Young people express the same kind of angst: "Our parents had everything set down for them in rules. We have to pick up ideas from all over and set our own. It's hard." Or this senior-high girl on the subject of marriage and human relationships: "'Forever' just isn't in my vocabulary."[16]

No matter what we do, the ultimate questions don't go away. Bibby's research reveals that though only one in three Canadians claims to relate to the church these days, fully 85% of the people he surveyed admit to asking questions about the meaning of life. More significantly, half of that 85% have given up expecting to find any answers.

In an effort to cope with the pressures brought on by changing lifestyles and continuing cultural anomie some people have sought out new forms of churching and living together. For a while during the 70's there were a host of informal "house churches" about. Others have experimented in new forms of communal living, seeking to create communities large enough to provide mutual support and yet small enough to preserve intimacy.

Grant Maxwell found that everywhere he went in Canada people expressed a preference for the local and near-to-hand over against the large and remote. In the dying days of second wave societies it becomes ever more difficult to organize a large mass of people around any external issue. This makes life difficult for those who would raise consciousness around issues of global justice. It also makes it increasingly difficult for traditional democratic societies to function. Such societies depend upon the existence of a solid middle consensus amongst the populace, a quality fast disappearing in the face of pluralism and fragmentation.

Even advertisers are becoming aware. It is becoming a major problem for them to target audiences large enough to justify the cost of the advertising. As the numbers of media channels proliferate within the developed world, the task of getting the unbeliever's ear becomes monumental. The problem is the same whether you want to interest the other in a new brand of soap or the gospel of Jesus Christ.

As the world moves into the 1980 s it discovers that industrialism is beginning to eat its own tail. It is spawning from within itself the forces of its own destruction. But it may, within a preverse providence of God, also be creating the new tools and thought-processes which may yet enable us to survive the third major wave of the human journey as it rolls in upon us.

Section IV

THE THIRD WORLD/
THIRD WAVE ASSAULT

Battle Grounds of the Future

1: Canadians, Caught in the Crossfire

It would be comforting if the watchman could reply
"Two a.m. and all's well!", but it would hardly be an ac-
curate description of the 1980 s. Not the least of the portents
on the horizon is the possibility that Canadians may already
be in the grip of the country's worst economic depression
since the 1920 s. At the conclusion of a recent TV interview
with the WCC's first general secretary, Dr. Wm. Visser
't Hooft, I asked for his predictions on the future of the
world church. He chuckled and declined, saying, "Every
time I've tried to predict the future, I've been wrong!"

All of the books on Canadian church history which I have
read in the past year quite naturally attempted to extrapolate
the future on the basis of trends current at the time of
writing—and most of them missed the boat! Books from the
'50s failed to forsee the impact of the Quiet Revolution in
Quebec. Books from the '60s naively predicted increasing
ecumenism and an ever-growing concern for global justice
issues. None of them anticipated the rapid secularization of
society, much less the collapse of industrialism itself.

One ends up having a good deal of sympathy for Jeremiah's
alter-ego, the prophet Hananiah. Hananiah too was simply
doing his best to read the signs of the times. Nor was it at all
clear to their contemporaries which of the two had God on
his side.

But one does not need to be particularly prophetic to ob-
serve that Canada's mainline churches are going into the
1980 s as a "disestablished minority" within their own
culture. Not since the days of the Clergy Reserves has
Canada had anything resembling a *legally* established church,
but the new experience is one of *cultural* disestablishment.
By and large the mainline churches have ceased to be the
glue of Canadian society. It is even questionable how effec-
tive they are being as yeast.

They are also discovering that at least one of the nation's
prophets of the '60s was right. Marshall McLuhan's global
village has arrived with a vengeance. What is done in one
place affects every place else. The problem is that there are
serious inequalities within the village. Some are still living,
literally, in a pre-First Wave nomadic existence (though such

are everywhere being squeezed almost into extinction).
Many others are primarily agricultural (first wave) in their
pattern of existence. Almost all of the globe's inhabitants
are being affected, one way or another, by the sheer dynamism
of the predominant Second Wave industrial culture. But increasingly the surge of a new Third Wave is about to overtake
the entire enterprise.

Too Much to Contemplate

The temptation for many is to dismiss the prophets of the
"third wave" as being modern-day Hananiahs. One
Tanzanian government official put it to me succinctly:
"Don't talk to me about satellites, microchips, and all of the
social ramifications you say will follow. We're still worrying
about clean drinking water in our villages and export
markets for our produce." For others, the prospect of
another industrial revolution (albeit a post-industrial one) is
simply too much to contemplate. It contradicts their
"blik." And if their blik includes a certain reluctance about
things North American, their rejection is the more complete;
because, for good or ill, it is in North America that the consequences of Third Wave technology and culture are most
evident.

If the world church really cares about its sisters and
brothers in North America it will have to take seriously this
fundamental aspect of the reality with which those brothers
and sisters are having to cope.

The speed of the change is overwhelming and it is much
more than a matter of new microelectronic gadgetry. There
are profound changes in the ways people interact with
one another, conduct their business transactions, and do
their playing together. The social dislocation affected by
the new technology has already begun, but for the most
part Canada's churches are as unprepared for this onslaught
as they were to deal with the causative forces behind the
1919 Winnipeg general strike.

The Chilean economist, Juan Rada, writing for the
International Labour Organization, makes it clear that not
just North Americans are in for some radical dislocation.

He says, "Today we are faced with micro-electronics, tomorrow bio-technology and, on the horizon, the substitution of materials; all three have profound implications for third world and industrialized countries alike. These issues will change the very fabric of society and the future of the social, cultural, economic and political life within countries in the international system."[17]

So no matter where one happens to be on the development spectrum one is faced with having to deal with the whole ball of wax; and the fact that we are at different points along that spectrum is a major part of the problem.

There are a few Canadians (primarily in the North) who are trying to preserve a nomadic lifestyle in the face of relentless Second and Third Wave incursions. There are others who are trying to maintain or revert to a more rural and agricultural life-style. But for the majority of Canadians their contemporary experience is one of being prodded into the open by the inexorable pressures of industrial society collapsing around them. Once there, they find themselves caught in a crossfire coming from the Third Wave on the one hand, and the Third World on the other. In such an exposed position vague memories of a once valid First Wave mythology provide precious little cover!

The temptation in the face of all this is to play Hananiah, who was after all a prophet of liberation. His prediction was that God would break the yoke of the people. Jeremiah, on the other hand, was one of those insufferable sufferers; he predicted that the existing wooden yokes would be replaced by iron ones.

The thought occurs that once again it may be God's intention that we should discover the Kingdom within the maelstrom, rather than by being able to see our way clearly through to the other side.

2: Third World Realities and Ambiguities

For concerned Canadian Christians one of the most anguishing aspects of the current apocalypse is the fact of the incredible differences in levels of material development between the members of the global family. If one is asked to serve on a national task force considering the possibilities of transmitting church audio-visual resources via satellite, one has not only to balance the request against other job commitments, the needs of family and personal sanity, but one has also to ask whether such a task should even be considered while there are refugee mothers and their children starving to death in Somalia, and people of conscience being tortured to death in country after country, all over the world.

But to opt totally for the latter can also be self-defeating. When I was in Geneva trying to prepare some video interpretations on the themes of the Sixth WCC Assembly, we had an almost impossible time piecing together bits of equipment from church resources. The Swiss Roman Catholics had given funds to a small ecumenical production centre, but the Protestants had not come up with their half of the funds because of a commitment to spend all their mission dollars on third world development. Frustrated, the centre's volunteer director appealed to the World Association for Christian Communicators only to be told, "But you're first world, you don't need funds from us!" Catch-22's abound. The people with the best private production facilities in the country turned out to be the Communist Party and the Divine Light Mission.

As a Canadian Christian I find it very difficult to live up to the biblical injunction to be "as innocent as doves and wise as serpents" when it comes to the stewardship, in the face of these differing global needs, of the talents and resources available to me. For in truth it seems that for all but a few saints, sharing is always relativized. Not many development workers would give up their telephones and photocopiers so that the poor might live better; and I know of at least one "people's leader" who has already picked out which airconditioned and carpeted office in the government hi-rise will be his when he comes to power.

So one begins to develop some compassion for the salesman

we met in the bar back at the beginning of this little book—he didn't want to let himself respond to the global needs coming at him in church and on TV because instinctively he knew that once you start to respond, the immensity and complexity of it all overwhelms you. You discover that there is indeed an angel with a flaming sword barring forever a return to the innocence of Eden once you have eaten of the tree of the knowledge of good and evil.

First Reactions

For most Canadian Christians the instinctive response to these global imbalances is a sense of guilt and a desire to try to help rectify the inequalities. Many of them give generously to development and aid programs of church, government and voluntary agencies. The Canadian government itself has taken a leading role of late in trying to equalize trade imbalances between the northern and southern hemispheres.

Many Canadians are trying to conserve resources and protect the ecosphere by driving smaller cars, re-insulating their homes, re-cycling waste, etc. Others are actively involved in political action lobbies of one kind or another dealing with human rights, refugees, and aid policies.

The vast majority of Canadians dislike American foreign policy, particularly as regards Latin America. Nor do Canadians indulge in the hysterical anti-Communism of the South Africans. The Communist Party and the Marxist-Leninists publish and propagandize as freely as anybody else in Canadian society. They regularly field candidates in Canadian elections and, significantly, rarely get them elected; a fact that needs to be taken seriously by those who wish to impose on Canada an analysis of the Canadian scene which is rooted in a different praxis.*

---

*Marxist theory cannot, at least for North America, explain (a) the fact that members of the same class are on opposite sides of some social conflicts, (b) the fact that the class system is itself complex and multi-layered in North America rather than easily divisible into two classes, the wealthy industrial elite and the workers, and (c) the fact that some forms of oppression in North America are not caused by class conflict, but by the conflict between geographical centres of power and their regional hinterlands. A multi-dimensional model, therefore, is needed to explain the North American social reality."[18]

But while Canadians do not instinctively brand Third World demands for a new deal as part of "a Communist conspiracy to destroy Christian civilization" there is nonetheless a growing feeling (even amongst church people) that they are getting tired of being scapegoated. After a while "Mea culpa, mea culpa" becomes more enervating than invigorating.

Canadians who have, after all, built a fairly successful society within the framework of capitalism, and who have evolved a functioning nation from a one-time colonial status, aren't convinced when others blame their troubles on, and attribute all of the world's systemic evil to, Western capitalism or the after-effects of a colonial legacy.

Now obviously most Canadians have a lot to learn about how such things as the international monetary system works to their advantage and to the disadvantage of others. But there would seem to be some validity to the observations that not only whites are racist, that Ugandans can behave cruelly towards fellow Ugandans, that Argentinians can manipulate and torture other Argentinians for their own ends, and that socialist governments can foul up too (eg: Poland).

The Size of the Global Village

Canadians for their part are having to come to terms with just how many other members there are of the global family. Even within the family of world Christians the probability is that by the year 2000 the majority will be non-Europeans, living in the southern hemisphere. At the start of this century only 3.5% of sub-Sahara Africa was Christian, whereas today it is 35% Christian. Much of the increase is due to the missionary efforts of indigenous African churches. Small wonder that, like the United Nations, the World Council of Churches is no longer a Western club.

Quite understandably, the rest of the world's peoples want a piece of the action. Last fall I attended a lecture with my friend the Kenyan bishop. It was given by the editor of a leading Southeast Asian economic journal. He told of a bullock cart which the UN and a host of development agencies had evolved for use in his part of the world. It was a marvel of intermediate technology: springs, rubber tires, the works. It was also somewhat more expensive than the traditional ox-cart but the agencies were very keen on its potential to improve the lot of the peasant farmers.

The foreign press was invited for a demonstration, at the end of which one of them asked the village headman if he had yet acquired one of the new carts. "Where would I get that kind of money?" replied the headman. Undaunted, the reporter pressed his case. "Suppose I gave you the money," he said, "would you then get one of these carts?" The villager thought for a moment and replied, "If you gave me that much money, I'd borrow the other half and buy a car." So much for intermediate technology.

To my surprise my Kenyan friend agreed with the headman. "We don't want second best," he told me, "we want what you've got." Which at best means that First Worlders will have to show that they too intend to live with less if they expect others to do so. At worst those words mean that everybody wants to be in on the rape of Mother Nature.

Canadians are experiencing some of these Third World pressures in the changing nature of immigration into their country. Canada has admitted some four million immigrants since 1967 and most of them have been, for the first time in the nation's history, *non*-European. Many have neither English nor French as their mother tongue; neither is Christianity their religion. Canada's predominantly Judeo-Christian society is having a hard time adjusting to the thought that there are now substantial numbers of Buddhist, Hindu and Muslim Canadians. Sometimes these new cultures do not blend easily with Canadian mythology. Arrogance and pride can exist on both sides and already there have been incidents of racial violence in Canada.

A vicious cycle is set in motion. Immigrants arrive from a country where they have had to push and jostle to secure a place in the sun. They run into enough put-downs in Canada to make them feel justified in continuing to do so. Canadians then resent their "pushiness." Add in elements of racism latent in the best of us and it isn't long before some otherwise placid Canadian is saying: "This is our country. If they don't like the way we do things let them go back where they came from." I was on a radio phone-in panel on the subject of racism when a caller used almost those exact words. The native Indian leader on the panel with me couldn't resist the dig. He nudged me in the ribs and whispered into my ear, "We've been trying to tell the rest of you that for 300 years!"

The View From Below

It is very difficult for North Americans, most of whom have never experienced grinding material poverty, to appreciate just how desperately poor so many of their fellows really are. Raymond Fung, WCC's Evangelism Secretary, makes the telling point that the Christian gospel must be a gospel for the materially poor, if for no other reason that there are so many of them. Given global realities, a gospel couched in a framework suited to the needs only of the well-to-do can hardly be a universal gospel.

What is most difficult for the average Canadian to grasp is his or her collusion in the suppression of others. Most Canadians felt positively towards their government's initiatives in events like the recent Cancun (Mexico) Conference on global trade. But a clue to the extent of the problem lies in the little reported fact that more than half of the world's population wasn't even invited to Cancun, for the simple and devastating reason that their share of global trade is too insignificant to matter.

Cancun turned out to be a meeting of the *old rich* (the industrialized North) and the *new rich* (OPEC) with the *prospectively rich* (Third Worlders on the way up). The agenda had to do with enlightened self-interest, for even the OPEC nations are realizing that money *per se* isn't of much use unless it is put into circulation. One has to get it into production, and that requires some paying customers at the end of the line. So it is simply in the best interests of the first two partners to get some purchasing power into the hands of the third.

Viewed in this light it should be no surprise to discover that most of the First World's foreign aid goes to those prospectively rich, middle-income nations. Only about one-third of the total aid finds its way to those in the bottom half of the pile. In essence it is global triage: triage being that activity whereby battlefield surgeons separate out the dying from the salvageable. And the Canadian economy is party to that process.

A few years ago the church in British Columbia invited a Third World visitor from the Dominican Republic to take part in its annual Ten Days for World Development. She made it crystal clear just how the international monetary system affects countries like her own:

> In 1908 the people of the Republic were in a First Wave economy. Land was communally owned, food was grown for local consumption and the people had enough to eat. Now 60% of the children die by the age of five. And all that changed was that the West's economy rolled in. The Cuban sugar crop went into decline in the late 19th century and the North American sugar companies shifted their operations to the Republic. Capital moved in and bought up the land. Soon the populace found itself growing sugar and raising beef for export on land where once people grew food to feed themselves.

Canadian prophets of social justice get very concerned about this state of affairs and very frustrated over the lack of comprehension evidenced by their countrymen. But the more strident become their eloquence and outrage, the more their peers in the comfortable pews simply tune them out. We have a serious communications problem on our hands, and one that is not about to be resolved by turning up the volume or increasing the amount of the rhetoric.

Different Worlds

At the heart of this communication gap there is a language problem caused by different political histories, and—most significant for Christians—differing experiences of the faith.

The language issue is the most obvious. Last year the Canadian Inter-Church Committee on Human Rights in Latin America came out of an intense week-end conference with a ringing declaration addressed to the Canadian churches. The problem was that while its language was faithful to the revolutionary struggle in Latin America, the consequence was exactly the opposite of what was intended. The declaration did not win Canadians to the cause. It simply turned them off. "Why?" Canadians asked themselves, "Why do revolutionaries have to use such 'slogans' and 'rhetoric'?"

As it turns out, there is a valid reason. Marxist communications analysts have rightly observed that the dominant group in any culture imposes its categories of thought upon everybody else in that society. Its ways of encoding information become the norm. This factor becomes extremely important when it comes to the storing of information in computer data banks. If the underdeveloped world is to participate at all in the world of the future, it needs easy access to such stored data. But information that to a third worlder is relevant and primary may seem irrelevant and secondary to those who control the encoding systems and devices. What the one might file under *"Liberation,* struggle for" the other might file under *"Terrorism,* suppression of", or worse—not bother storing at all.

In order to break a cycle of dominance which they find to be intolerable, many third world liberationists have deliberately opted for a style of analysis which has its own set of encoding categories based on reading history as a dialectical process, essentially of class struggle. In such a system, history is seen primarily as an interplay between oppressors and victims; and for all too many in today's world that is an appropriate analysis.

But like any human convention, that analysis has its limitations. In terms of language its consequence is that one ends up unable to communicate with those who do not share one's praxis. Ultimately both sides end up simply speaking past each other, unable—sometimes unwilling—to hear and understand the perspective from which the other speaks.

Consider, that people who are having to wrest from landowners and oppressive governments the right of free expression will probably find it very difficult to believe the Canadian experience in which, for instance, the government has mandated that the owners of TV cable systems must provide a community access channel, complete with production facilities, available to any in the community who feel they have something important to say. Conversely, I have witnessed in North America some incredibly inane interviews of important third world leaders, conducted by Western journalists who were so locked into their own little world-view that their questions had absolutely no relevance whatsoever to the realities from which their guests had come.

Gustavo Guitierrez, that major prophet of liberation theology, puts the contrast neatly when he observes that the poor of Latin America will, out of their experience, opt always for "... social revolution rather than reform, liberation rather than social development, (and) socialism rather than liberalization."[19] He may very well be describing his situation with deadly accuracy. But the point to be made here is that the average Canadian would choose precisely the second of those options in every case; and furthermore is tired of being put down for doing so. If the goal of the liberation struggle is "political power at the service of the great popular majorities," most Canadians would affirm that, in essence, that's what they already have.

The language issue is not an easy one to overcome. But it would be a move in the right direction to acknowledge that there is more than one praxis within which to evaluate reality, more than one way of describing what's going on in God's universe. God may be more in some situations than in others, but He still sits in judgement upon all of our human salvation formulas.

Differing Political Perceptions

But such a plea reveals the political problem in the first world/third world communications gap, namely the age-old split between classic liberalism and uni-dimensional radicalism (whether of the right or of the left). Canada's origins, its history, and its experience under industrialism, have all inclined its citizenry towards a pluralistic liberalism which presumes a variety of possible resolutions to any particular human dilemma. This leads to an inevitable clash with "one-wayers," no matter what their stripe or their cause.

On reflection there is a rather frightening similarity between John Calvin, Adolf Hitler, Josef Stalin, George Fox,

Senator McCarthy, and Juan de Torquemada. All of them were absolutely convinced that their way, and only their way, was correct. One commentator summed up all such recently with the observation that "in their heart of hearts, most of them are incapable of believing that anyone of intelligence and goodwill does not really, at bottom, agree with them."[20]

The slogans vary. For one it is "Send in the Marines!" For another, "Drown the Witch!" or "Down with the Imperialist Reactionairies!" or even, "Jesus! Jesus! Jesus!" The end results are often tragically similar. The conviction carries the struggle well, but it turns the victors into tyrants. One of my favourite Canadian theologians is fond of observing that "righteousness in a vacuum, is a monster."

Take even two of the cardinal tenents of liberation theology:

"Liberation theology has maintained that active commitment to liberation comes *first...*"[21]

and

"Liberation theology's second central intuition is that God is a liberating God, revealed *only* in the concrete historical context of liberation of the poor and oppressed. This second point is inseparable from the first." (italics mine).[22]

Useful, even necessary, tools in the human struggle for the just, participatory and sustainable world order these principles undoubtedly are. But the italic words suggest that there is the potential for idolatry even here. To put anything other than God first and to presume God has only one sphere of legitimate action is, perhaps, to presume too much.

The World Council of Churches' most serious image problem in North America is that it is not seen as daring to make that kind of critique of liberation thought from within. Such analyses are left to the Ernest Lefevres of this world, people whose stake in the status quo is so obvious that their criticisms can easily be brushed aside. The tragedy is that a populace bereft of any other tools for coming to terms with an unbearable collective guilt seizes on such shallow but available critiques as a way out.

On Capitalism

It may even be time for somebody in the churches to dare to say a word on the brighter side of capitalism; for some of those talking most loudly about global economic reform and a redistribution of global assets simply have no idea just how hard it is "to make a buck:" to acquire capital, risk it and manage it so as to generate the wealth of a society.

It seems fairly obvious that if one wants to be in on industrialism one has to acquire capital. And to get capital somebody has to abstain from consumption, or input labour for which they do not take back total compensation. It takes a brave political leader to say: "We must sacrifice now and do without, so that our children may live better." Especially when it is likely that the generation of children will be like most Canadians are today—lavishly spending and barely replenishing the stock of capital built up by the sacrifices of their parents and grandparents.

But capital—even capitalism—is not a dirty word. Karl Marx (who invented the term) knew that. Without it there is no Second Wave and no Third Wave either.

Differing Faith Experiences

One of the principal reasons why Third World and North American Christians have a hard time hearing one another is that their faith histories are so different. Reading Guitierrez one begins to appreciate the extent to which liberation theology is a reaction against a theological classicism, against a preoccupation with ontological abstractions and other-worldly asceticism. For sensitive and compassionate Christians surrounded by human misery and degradation, such an approach to the faith finally became unpardonable. They found themselves encountering the living God in the concrete realities of the struggle for liberation and justice.

North American mainline Christians, on the other hand, have lived with, worked at, and been fed on the social gospel for the past 100 years. Which is not to say that they changed the world as a result—but it is to say that many of them are both suspicious of its ability to ultimately deliver what it promises, and hungry for an experience of the transcendent God. Some of them are actively pursuing such traditional spiritual disciplines as prayer, meditation, and fasting.

It is not hard to understand why some of the radicalized Third World Christians view such a development with suspicion. To them it looks very much like an attempt to escape into the kind of other-worldly pietism from which they have just removed themselves, which is of course the demonic potential of such yearnings. But it can also lead to a new appreciation of the source of Christian empowerment. Nor is the historical struggle free of its own kind of demons.

North American Christians, for their part, cannot let their spiritual quest ignore the harsh realities of global injustice nor the evils of the present world order. There can be no words but judgment on the West's boycott of the struggling democracy in Nicaragua (which Victoria's Bishop Remi de Roo has said is the last chance for a Christian revolution in Central America). The same holds true of Western responses to the reconstruction efforts in Vietnam.

The Eyes of the Victim

Western Christians cannot play armchair moralists in the face of the repeated evidence that it usually takes an armed revolutionary struggle to overcome the tyranny of vested interests. My parents were for many years in Zimbabwe (then Rhodesia) so I am all too aware that the whites there (with a few notable exceptions, most of whom were church people) did not even consider sharing political power with the country's blacks until they were confronted by guerrilla armies on their doorsteps. Telling conflicting interests in such situations to sit down and negotiate, when one of them holds all the face-cards and is playing with a marked deck, is hardly a Christian thing to do.

In the face of such differing perceptions of God and his world Christians are called to love that world and each other. Perhaps their deepest sin is their unwillingness to understand and honour each other's pilgrimage. Mortimer Arias, the Bolivian Methodist bishop now living in exile in the USA, keeps urging his students to look at others with compassion. "Jesus always looked through the eyes of the victim," he says, "and everybody is a victim one way or another." If such an approach worked on Bishop Arias' jailers surely it is appropriate for Christians seeking to communicate their passion for a better world to one another.

The Micro-Chip is Here to Stay

3: Third Wave Coming On

Very few church people, even in a developed nation like Canada, have yet grasped the speed with which devastating technological change is bearing down upon them. It is estimated that if airline travel had advanced technically on the same scale since 1950 as has microelectronics, we would today be crossing the Atlantic in ten minutes, at a cost of about two cents, travelling in something the size of a shoebox!

Consider that today 100,000 bits of information can be packed on one electronic "chip" the size of a little fingernail. In the early 1960s the density was ten per chip. By 1990 it will be one million.

Fortunately there is a generation coming along that understands what's going on. Just after Alvin Toffler's book *The Third Wave* was published, a friend got hold of a copy. She left in on the kitchen counter overnight. Next morning her 17-year-old, out-of-school, out-of-work teenage son bounded down the stairs with the book in his hand. He had stayed up all night and read it through. His comment was significant: "Mom," he said, "I've got a future after all."

Toffler offers a wide-ranging analysis of the evolution and shape of post-industrial society. The industrial pressures of massification, concentration and synchronization, etc., are, he says, already reversing themselves. In the world of electronic cottage industries, "small" becomes not only

beautiful but exceedingly practical. In an information age the creative handling of information becomes more important than working on a production line (which is better run by computerized robots anyway). He points out that at today's automobile and gasoline prices it doesn't take long to pay off the cost of a home-based computer terminal simply out of savings from the cost of commuting.

Brave New World?

Two-way coaxial cable is already in place in many parts of North America, so it is not a pipe-dream to consider both parents conducting many of their business and household affairs from the home, with only occasional trips to an office, shopping centre or factory. Many people in North America are already doing so. The idea of children doing much of their school work on flex time via home video modules sounds bizarre but the models are already active. And these technological marvels that bring information to people are far more ecologically sound than our present practice of moving the people to the information (on congested highways and into crowded urban cores).

To businesses in Canada the benefits of the electronics revolution are already apparent. Sales of word processors and small computers have skyrocketed. Last year our Church's annual provincial conference put its registration procedures on a computer and as a result breezed through the whole time-consuming process. One of my acquaintances at the First Global Futures Conference (Toronto 1980) was an executive with a Canadian communications company. Each afternoon he would go to his hotel room, plug his computer terminal into the phone line, read his in-basket in his office 2000 miles away, deal with the items (calling additional information out of file memory if needed), then file the completed transactions in his out-basket for his staff to deal with the next morning. Not only did he come home after a trip to find everything up to date, but he and staff could then spend their time together talking, thinking, planning and being, rather than spend their time rushing around trying to catch up on a back-log of detail work.

What's more, the cost of all this hardware is actually coming down. In 1965 the average cost of installing a phone circuit was $22,000, by 1985 it will be only $30. Ground receivers for satellite transmissions that originally cost upwards of $10 million apiece, are now available for only $200. Even underdeveloped nations need to think twice before rejecting as superficial frills all this accoutrement of the Third Wave, for such hardware may hold the key to their future.

Rough Water Ahead
But the interval between cross and resurrection is going to be very rough going indeed. It is difficult enough for the already industrialized nations. Jobs once considered secure (from linotype operators, to car manufacturing, to office clerking) become suddenly redundant. Those laid off from

the assembly lines of Detroit and Oakville (auto manufacturing) seldom have the kinds of skills needed in "Silicon Valley", California (microtechnology manufacturing). Centralized data processing, done by parent companies in the USA, has already cost Canada some 23,000 jobs and billions of dollars in revenue in the accounting and data-coordinating fields alone. The changes are major and they are now.

For the Third World, Third Wave technology is even more of a mixed blessing. On the one hand it promises information, readily available, which would otherwise take years to compile. But the big question is, who will control the data banks and how will they assemble the information? Since the research and development costs for the hardware are astronomical, it is unrealistic to expect its developers to readily make it available to "poor" countries.

If the data banks remain in the control of the developed countries, the costs of gaining access to them will become a heavy drain on scarce foreign exchange reserves in the developing nations. Juan Rada's advice to his fellows in the third world[23] is that they invest now in some of the hardware and develop their own data banks before the dependence on First World resources becomes irreversible. In which connection it is interesting to note that on April 6, 1982, India launched two communications satellites of its own, and has manufactured its own ground hardware to go with them.

There are serious repercussions in the market place as well, where Third World countries stand to lose one of their few trump cards, namely cheap labour. High technology makes it profitable for the North to bring some of its labour-intensive industries back to home soil. On the other hand, while industrialized nations leapfrog over one another in a race for micro-electronics supremacy, they are leaving behind some high technology equipment which is far from obsolete and which developing nations can pick up at bargain prices. Not only can this equipment help restore the latter to a competitive position; it can also add to their capital revenues by reducing skill training in critical areas which can now be handled by the new hardware. But the whole enterprise demands enormous foresight and energy, plus a willingness on the part of the developed nations to share generously from the new bag of goodies.

How Will the Churches Respond?

One would like to dream that the churches would be in the vanguard of this new wave of human development. One imagines them understanding it and helping others to do so; using it creatively (think of the savings in travel costs if many of our church meetings were done via computer conferencing); critiquing it fearlessly. But alas, the late John Taylor seems to have been right when he noted that the churches still do not believe anything has been communicated unless it has been enshrined in print, in multiple copies, on pink, green or white paper.

Binary logic is not taught in seminaries and few sermons are preached on Third Wave living. How then will the churches expect to have a role in calling the new science and technology before the bar of human hopes and aspirations? For called to the bar it must be. Its hardware and infrastructures are no more neutral than were their industrial wave counterparts and predecessors.

Strangely enough, that emerging concern of North American mainline religion to rediscover right-brain experiences of God may not be as far off the mark as its critics imagine. For it is becoming apparent that it will not be the technocrats who will determine the uses to which microtechnology will be put. Rather it will be the systems thinkers, the visionaries, those who are able to think (w)holistically in patterns, those who are able to conceptualize relationships and meanings between the otherwise disconnected bits and pieces of information which can be stored—almost ad infinitum—in the steel and plastic coffins of the computer's memory.

In other words, you don't have to know how the insides of the computer work in order to use it creatively. In fact the irony is that the more one understands the linear-functioning innards, the more limiting that is apt to be to one's creative potential! At precisely this juncture people who can address the large issues of the meaning of human existence may be the most valuable people one can have around.

But if the people of God consume most of their energy in resisting their Creator's call to these new arenas of service, there will be plenty of others—with perhaps baser motives—waiting to move into the void.

"All the King's Horses..."

4:The Collapse of the Second Wave World

"Couldn't put Humpty together again." So runs the old nursery rhyme about the egg that fell off the wall. The one thing none of us can do is to go back to the good old days of the heyday of the industrial revolution. The old order is in serious trouble everywhere one looks:

*What really bothers me is that I'm more radical than they are. I know the system's had it. All they can think about is their pensions. (*A wealthy Canadian financier, regarding the reactions of church officials to her proposals regarding church funding.)

We are in the process of killing an old civilization and creating a new one. (Alvin Toffler addressing a college symposium, December 1981).

The faith of an entire epoch is coming to an end in our era. (Hans Kung, at a theological convocation, December 1981).

It was in life-style changes that the cracks in industrialism's infrastructures first appeared back in the '60s, but the '80s crunch is coming in the economic sphere. In the West interest rates rise to an unprecedented 20%. In Poland food prices are jacked up 400% in an effort to save the ship of state. Several underdeveloped countries could cause a panic in world banking circles simply by telling their creditors: "OK, we give up. So repossess us!"

Both Great Britain and the USA have tried to remedy the situation by ditching Keynesian economics and opting for an older supply-side model. Such simple faith in Say's Law (i.e. that supply will create demand) is touching, but seems to ignore the fact that people need something with which to buy if the system is to work at all. The original supply-side economists assumed a labour market capable of ensuring full employment. One of Keynes' great contributions was to prove that such was not the case. The futurist Robert Theobald now maintains with some forcefulness that full employment is not even any longer desirable—its impact on the ecosphere would be disastrous.

What none of the earlier market economists foresaw was the way in which oligopolies (three or four large firms controlling a given market) would come to dominate the world's economy. In such a situation none of the traditional monetary controls seem to work (lowering the money supply, raising the interest rates, etc.). The only certain consequences of restraints now is that the oligopolies immediately cut back on production. Thus the vicious downward spiral commences and the very last thing to drop is prices—which were supposed to be the first item to come down.

So the system grinds on until even the oligopolies grow top heavy and topple over—only to be propped up again by governments that don't dare consider the implications of a world in which a bicycle and a home computer might be a more efficient investment than putting another Chrysler in the garage.

Meanwhile big education continues to crank out university graduates for whom there are no jobs. Big armies build up nuclear warheads which no sane person could conceive of using. Big industry, running out of things to invest in, buys up little industries. A system predicated upon growth finds itself confronted by limits to growth and even in affluent Canada the message comes clear—Humpty just isn't going to go back together.

At the end of 1981, unemployment in Canada had created

a horde of jobless greater than the ranks of the nation's armed services during the Second World War. Welfare rates, inadequate at the best of times, are overwhelmed by the inflation rate; the Unemployment Insurance Fund is so close to bankruptcy that nobody knows quite what to do about it. The '60s spawned a great many single-parent families in Canada, most of them headed by women. Now fully 41% of the female-led households in the country are living below the poverty line.

For many Canadians the 1980 s are proving to be what the editor of the nation's leading news magazine has called "a time of anarchic impulses and lost touchstones." Small wonder so many, particularly the young and the unskilled, are tempted to forsake the national myths and give in to the creeping paralysis of despair.

The Retreat to the Right

5: First Wave Nostalgia

But there are still significant numbers of people who, while rejecting both Third World pressures and Third Wave realities, are not about to give up on the "good life" once delivered by the engine of industrialism. Their response to the conflicting pressures of the age is to return with a vengeance to a reinforcing of the monomyths of a simpler, more glorious era. And this collective trip down memory lane is swinging inexorably to the political, cultural and religious right.

By and large mainline religious groups both in Canada and the USA have failed to take the matter anywhere near seriously enough. They pick away at the phenomenon of the electronic evangelists from the heights of a supposed theological superiority while the Moral Majority unseats political liberals and single-issue lobbyists take over the hospital boards. Hardly a mainline congregation in Canada has a Sunday evening service of any kind. But the Alliance and Pentecostal churches are jammed on Sunday evenings— mainly by young people.

The new fundamentalist right stresses *personal* salvation. This has always been the principal thrust of North American revivalism but it has a particularly strong impact on a populace that has been privatized by industrial society. The new revivalism is rooted in a *Biblicism* which, while it is woefully selective in its choice of scriptural proof-texts, nonetheless claims for those texts an absolute authority. To an anchorless people such assurances have an almost irresistible appeal.

Whereas mainline Christians tend to see *humanists and pluralists* as allies against the dehumanizers of this world, the new religious right sees such folk as the arch enemy. And while traditional denominations are busy campaigning against human rights violations in Korea and South Africa, the religious right is lobbying to get sex out of television programming. And their threatened boycott of TV advertisers has got results that make the mainliners' lettuce and Nestles boycotts look like a tempest in a teapot.

Liberal Christians don't much like the tactics of these new zealots but, as Jim Wall of *The Christian Century* points out, it was the liberals who taught them how to do it. The fundamentalists just apply the techniques more ruthlessly and with quicker results. The religious right has entered into politics in the USA with a vengeance. It has campaigned with considerable success against Equal Rights for Women, for the banning of homosexuals from the classrooms, for the cutting of welfare rates, and for an increase in "defense" spending. It's done in the name of God and the "American Way," which awakens disquieting ghosts from the last days of Germany's Weimar Republic.

Born again religion does not yet exercise that kind of

political clout in Canada, and Canada's leading religious TV talk-show is a much gentler example of the genre than some of its American counterparts. But it should be noted that the most mail—on any subject—which Joe Clark received while he was Prime Minister of Canada, was over the government regulating agency's refusal to grant a broadcasting license to a right-wing religious group.

At a time when most of the mainline denominations are cutting their communications departments to the bone, the religious right is entering the field of electronic evangelism with energy, dollars, know-how and commitment. Some of the results are dreadful. What is being propagated in the name of Jesus on North American air-waves is at times frightening. But they are reaching people while we are clucking our tongues.

As the retreat to the right gathers momentum, the great cultural monomyths, so bloodied by the disaster of Vietnam, rise phoenix-like from their graves and into them is breathed new life. Almost fanatically they are reaffirmed, and those who would ask about their appropriateness to a new time are brushed to one side or branded as communists. To the old myths is added a dimension of Apocaplypse with the assertion that God will not let his beloved fall by the wayside. Resurrection will come—if not this side of nuclear holocaust, then certainly on the other.

It is a potent brew. And one in which a real-live Jeremiah or Jesus would be an unwelcome tune-out factor.

Section V

THE CHALLENGE FOR THE CHURCHES

Raft, Wind and Sail

1: Some Home Truths
About the Canadian Church

In the face of all this, where exactly do the churches of Canada stand? Parts of that answer have already been alluded to: a disestablished minority in a secular culture, struggling with third world pressures, barely cognizant of third wave potentials, parts of it feeling a vigorous nostalgia, much of it holding the line, some of it showing occasional outbursts of creative discipleship.

In the pronouncements of their church courts and governing bodies Canada's mainline denominations are supporters of the contemporary WCC stance, committed to the search for a just, sustainable and participatory world order. But the reality in the congregations is somewhat more basic. There you find more of the spectrum hinted at in our five opening scenarios.

Very few Canadians go to church because it is the socially accepted thing to do (as it once was), or because it is good for business (it's not much good for that anymore either!). But one of the principal reasons why many people I know participate in their local congregation is because it is one of the few centres of genuine caring and real community in an increasingly soulless social environment. There is a lot of mutual ministry going on in the average Canadian congregation, which must surely gladden the heart of God.

The nurturing encourages exploration into the great questions which the faith seeks to address. Bible study groups have come into their own with renewed vigour during the past five to ten years—so have prayer groups and charismatic renewal movements, even a renewed interest in the power of spiritual healing.

I am always amazed at the incredible loyalty of so many ordinary Christians, who remain faithful to their Lord and to the best of a remembered tradition even when they neither understand nor agree with some of the positions taken by the institutional church and/or its leadership. I further believe that there is more hard-nosed ethical decision-making going on in the comfortable pews than the inhabitants thereof are usually credited with. And many of the people who are sustaining the social fabric and volunteer-life of their communities are the same ones who are turning up in church on Sunday mornings.

There are also some who find their church congregation to be a stimulus for exploring global realities and a platform from which to engage with others in an assault upon the principalities and powers of this world. But my hunch is that they are a minority. Certainly their popular support is neither as great nor as uncritically given as it was a decade ago. "A mighty army whose marshalled ranks await the call to battle," would not spring to one's lips as a description of the Canadian mainline churches at this point in their history!

Still, all of this represents an enormous reservoir of good will waiting to be tapped for the global mission of Christ's church in our day. But manipulating the collective guilt of this marvellously varied collection of "saints" is not the way to release all that potential. Some words of grace, understanding and forgiveness might be worth a try.

Grant Maxwell came back from his travels across the nation impressed not by its institutions, but by the quiet strength and commitment of individual Canadians; ordinary decent folk, none of whom would set the world on fire but all of whom knew how to be faithful in small things.

Even on the institutional level there are small signs of hope. The Inter-church Coalition on Corporate Responsibility, after eight years of patiently raising global justice and human rights issues at the annual meetings of corporations in which the churches own stock, in 1982 was able to persuade 9% of Alcan Aluminum's shareholders to join in asking for a review of the corporation's business investments in South Africa. Hardly a world-shattering event, but at least an indicator of the worth of persistence. And who can tell which way the mood of anti-nuclear protest will go? Indeed who would dare to predict what God might be able to do with all that collective faithfulness?

2: Back to Basics

Dr. Hans Kung has made the point that in our era even some of the traditional categories of thought within which faith questions have for centuries been framed, are open to question.

Certainly Canadian Christians (along with their fellow Christians everywhere) are finding themselves pressured by the forces of change to re-ask some fundamental questions about God, life and their own monomyths. Deep down they are asking, *are we going to make it* (or *is the world going to self-destruct*)? Many, their Sunday School faith shaken by the events of the past two decades, are asking if they have yet really understood the Gospel. Like Humphrey Bogart (in the movie *Casablanca*) they are saying, *Play it again, Sam* (or *Tell me the Stories of Jesus*—once again). Finally, their tidy definitions of an orderly and predictable God in disarray, they are once more asking the ultimate religious question, *Who are you really, God?*

Are We Going To Make It?

I grew up during the Second World War. But I was safely tucked away in the wilds of northern Quebec where it was easy to believe that God would always see to it that ultimately righteousness (our side) prevailed. I doubt I was ever taught that. I suspect I just picked it up by osmosis. In the theology of contemporary right-wing evangelicalism that belief is still prevalent.

However one chooses to understand God's omnipotence, there is a mountain of evidence to suggest that that is a naive and mistaken belief. God seems to take human freedom very seriously, and does not in fact suspend his own ground rules to save us from the consequences of our own global insanity.

Thousands of God's most conscientious and concerned servants have been tortured and abused during the past decade in prisons all over the world. God may have become very real to those being persecuted, but the point is that the torture goes on nonetheless. Read the files of Amnesty International (or the World Council of Churches for that matter) and you begin to understand the stridency of those voices asking that the rest of us *do* something about such a state of affairs.

I watched recently a television programme on the subject of nuclear proliferation and was appalled that the majority of the studio audience seemed to believe that God would somehow intervene if humanity was on the verge of turning the globe into a nuclear incinerator. This is a subject close to the heart of any Canadian. If it ever does get down to a shootout between the super-powers, it is the skies above Canada that will host the fireworks display.

History seems to be telling us that such "faith" is a cop-out. God seems to be an incorrigible gambler who has decided that the potential benefits to us are worth the risk of the gift of human freedom. There is no evidence that God has ever forced himself upon the human experience. Not even in Jesus. We are free to tell even him to go away. It is conceivable that we may yet blow ourselves up unless we take steps to prevent it.

This is a serious assault on the Canadian monomyth that anyone, by hard work and sacrifice, can make it. None of us may make it. Certainly none of us can anymore make it on our own. A changing world order is forcing Canadians out of their comfortable individualism and into an awareness of the meaning of *solidarity*. It also places a new sense of urgency and poignancy on the old Quaker dictum that when it comes to ending the torture system and stopping the arms race, "God has no hands but thine." The answer to the question "Will we make it?" seems to depend in large measure on what we do about it.

Play It Again, Sam

At one point in her life my mother helped to write the first all-Africa Sunday School curriculum. She recounts the difficulty they had in writing Easter lessons on a continent where Easter comes in the fall, not the spring. They found themselves bereft of all those obvious symbols of new life springing up from the seemingly dead seeds all around.

For the first time in their experience Canadian Christians are being asked to do the same thing—to conceive, believe and articulate the gospel at a time when they are surrounded by more outward evidence of death than of life.

It was easy to be part of a resurrection faith in an era of unlimited possibilities for growth. From time to time the cause might seem to be suffering setbacks, but with a little more energy and commitment, goodness would win the day eventually. Now it becomes obvious that the gospel had better be more than that, or it is simply not worth hanging on to. So play it again, Sam; run it past me one more time.

Most of us in the West have assumed that the gospel story is essentially *comedy*— in the sense that the hero ultimately triumphs. Now we are being forced to ask if it might not instead be *tragedy,* even the *theatre of the absurd.*

God and history have conspired to force us back upon paradox; to an acknowledgement that the gospel is *both* resurrection and crucifixion, *both* comedy and tragedy, held in an impossible creative tension. For the Christian the ultimate truth about life becomes a paradox, with God at the end of it.

Parable theology contends that such a paradox is precisely the objective of all evangelistic activity, uniquely modelled by Jesus himself. It is not a matter of trying to sell somebody a complete package; rather it is the constant precipitation of encounters with the paradox of God in the hope that the responder might thereby "tumble" into the Kingdom, into the Presence.

That comes as a very revolutionary thought to someone whose orientation has been to *build* the Kingdom of God—on Earth. Our very inability to pull that off makes us ask if there are not other ways of viewing the question. The third wave, with its emphasis on *kairos* rather than *chronos* time, helps us to investigate the possibility that our preoccupation with an historical time-line (with the Kingdom of God as the end point) may be a partial understanding of the matter.

The social gospel, liberation theology, even fundamentalist apocalypticism all tend to think of the Kingdom in terms of linear time. But many religious and philosophical systems (eg: Hinduism, Buddhism, Existentialism, native Canadian religion) sit very loose to the importance of chronological time. Now there are biblical scholars like Gerhard Von Rad who tell us that Jesus and the prophets did too.

The weary crusaders of this world are invited to discover that experiences of the Kingdom can be much more immediate, personal and even transitory than they had supposed. Jesus went about announcing that the Kingdom of God was involved in every human decision, and that at any given moment any individual could be in it, out of it, or not far from it!

None of which necessarily denies the possibility of a consummation to history. But it does take some of the angst out of the striving for it. Good news for a disestablished cultural minority in an uncertain world.

Who Are You Really, God?

I grew up with a very predictable God—a very kind one to be sure, but, in retrospect, a rather tame one. The collapse of the world view that shaped that understanding forces me to ask if there might be more to God than what I have so far experienced.

It's hard to get a handle on God. The very attempt to form images of Him is partly an exercise in idolatry, since idolatry is the setting up of anything less than God (e.g. one's mental image) in the place of God! Indeed, the nobler the substitute (the better the image, the closer it is to the "real thing"), the more demonic its potential. One sympathizes with the school child who limited her description of God to "sort of an oblong blur."

Idolatry also tends to limit the essential element of paradox, for it leads us to shape God into definable packages, neatly wrapped and labelled in doctrines, dogmas and creeds. The golden metaphors get melted down into golden calves, and thus lose their ability to prod us beyond ourselves and into encounter with the genuine article. Occasionaly we even presume to announce what "we know to be the will of God for the church" or to lay out time-lines for "God's plan of salvation." Fortunately God seems to have so constructed us that even when all of our tired metaphors have been cast in bronze and approved by our solemn assemblies, the hungering for an experience of the living God remains.

Sometimes, especially in the middle of apocalypse, the temptation is to wish that God would be a little more obvious about his nature and expectations of us. But at the end of the day, all we really have is Jesus. And there the trick is to let the Parable work without making an idol out of him too.

I spent eight years doing Open Line radio in Canada. We were on the air on Sunday mornings while the Christians were at church because we wanted to dialogue with the people who weren't. We listened to a lot of hostile people during those years. Many of them were really "down" on the church, but significantly, almost all of them liked Jesus. He came to them out of the pages of the New Testament, sometimes in spite of the Gospel writers (whose own need for a champion seems frequently to have turned Jesus into a master debater, excelling at brilliant repartee and the putting down of Pharisees and Saducees).

Now New Testament scholarship is helping us to see that the reality was probably much simpler, and a great deal more appealing. This deeply religious and passionate man was, primarily, a teller of parables; a story teller in the village markets. Taking the every-day experiences of every-day people and turning their every-day expectations upside down with a "What if...?"

What if ... the landlord's son came to claim the vineyard and the tenants threw him out? What if ... the wastrel son came home to a feast and the loyal son got nothing? What if ... those who tried to lynch a prophet found him giving his life of his own free will? What if ... the Messiah should suffer a criminal's execution? Small wonder the cross ended up as foolishness to the Greeks and a stumbling block to the Jews.

Who are you really, God? What if ... we couldn't understand the answer even if we found it? Paradox and parable, and at the end of the day all we have is Jesus. But as even my agnostic radio listeners were aware, that's not a bad place to start.

3: Facing the Apocalypse

While I was completing this book in Geneva, people kept asking me to describe what the churches in Canada are doing to meet the challenges of the '80s. I hope a partial answer has at least been alluded to in the preceding sections. As far as I can see, the institutional church is doing what it has always done—a bit of this and a bit of that. Some of it good and some of it not. The times are not tidy and apt to get messier. Apocalyptic times are not conducive to large-scale institutional innovation.

But the institution does provide the supportive framework for the people and, like Grant Maxwell, I am convinced that that is where the real strength of both the church and the nation lies. Furthermore it seems to me that those individuals could use a new paradigm within which to approach their ministry.

John Dominic Crossan, the Roman Catholic New Testament scholar[24] suggests that we should abandon some of our traditional paradigms: seeing life as a battle to be won, or a task to be completed. The better metaphor for life, he says, is the metaphor of *game*, something to be entered into for its own sake and something which by definition, can never be "achieved". (A game which can be played perfectly every time ceases to be fun, and the players have to seek out something more challenging.)

Life, the experience of God's Kingdom, is—he says—to be found in the coping, not in the arriving; in the game, rather than in the victory. It is like sailing close-hauled into the wind, lee rail under, spray flying and playing for every ounce of headway you can get.

I was part of a World Council event in British Columbia's Naramata Centre some five years ago that experienced the truth of Crossan's model. We had gathered from all over the world, leaders of Christian lay training academies, to examine ways of using the Bible more creatively in our various training programmes.

While we were there the world fell apart around us. The very first morning brought news that the South African government had banned almost all the mixed-racial groups in the country. Several of those in our midst were directly affected, uncertain even if they dared to return home. The following day a similar fate befell the Koreans. The third day brought news of the "suicides" in the West German police cells of persons known to some members of our company. All week long we were surrounded with more and more bad news.

As we sought to understand Jesus' words about his ministry—to preach good news to the poor, recovery of sight to the blind, liberty to the oppressed—we were faced with evidence of defeat all around us. Where was the Kingdom Jesus was so enthusiastically proclaiming?

Then, on our very last day together, we gradually became aware that we had been shifted into the presence of the ultimate. Finally we understood that we had in fact been in the Kingdom all week as we had agonized over our uncertainties and fears. God, Creator and Redeemer, had come to us in the midst of the storm, not to still the waters but rather to help with the sails!

Once Shadrach, Meshach and Abednego accepted the fact that there was no escaping the fiery furnace, they suddenly found themselves able to sing about it. Crossan suggests that our experience may be not so much a fiery furnace as a life-raft. A survival kit for the 1980s could be shaped around the thought that all the world's a raft and all of us its passengers. In the midst of the raft is God the Parabler, patiently breaking open our tidy solutions to our dilemmas, always pushing us toward the edge—where God the Creator awaits us with the invitation to come sailing, on the winds of God!

I feel the winds of God today,
Today my sail I lift,
Though heavy oft with drenching spray
And torn with many a rift;
If hope but light the water's crest,
And Christ my bark will use,
I'll seek the seas at his behest,
and brave another cruise....

(Jessie Adams—
The United-Anglican Hymnal
No. 282)

JESUS CHRIST · THE LIFE OF THE WORLD

NOTES

Number	Page	Source
1	25	Knight, James, (Ed), *"Canada, The Formative Years,"* *Imperial Oil Review,* July 1976, p. 29
2	32	Walsh, H.H., *The Christian Church in Canada,* (Ryerson, Toronto, 1956), p. 137
3	38	Knight, p. 77
4	39	Walsh, p. 229
5	46	Broadfoot, Barry, *The Pioneer Years, 1895-1914,* (Doubleday Canada, 1976), p. 38.
6	47	Ibid., p. 9.
7	48	Ibid., p. 42.
8	60	Roddan, Sam, *Batter My Heart,* (United Church of Canada, Vancouver 1975) p. 28
9	62	Colden, Cadwallader, quoted in *Canada's Illustrated Heritage Series* (ed- Pierre Berton), (Natural Science of Canada Ltd., Toronto, 1978), Vol V.
10	67	Roddan, p. 97
11	80	Maxwell, Grant, *Signs and Portents of the Seventies,* (Canadian Catholic Conference, 1975).
12	82	Bibby, Reginald, *"The State of Collective Religiosity in Canada,"* *Canadian Review of Sociology and Anthropology,* (February 1979), and Oliver, Dennis, *"The New Canadian Religious Plurality,"* 1979
13	86	Maxwell, Vol III A, p. 9.
14	86	Ibid, p. 9.
15	86	Ibid, p. 12.
16	92	Ibid.
17	92	Rada, Juan F., *"The Microelectronics Revolution: Implications For the Third World,"* *Development Dialogue* (2/1982), pps. 41-67. p. 44.
18	94	Crockett, W.R., *"Political Theology In British Columbia"* *The Ecumenist,* Vol 20, No. 1 (November 1981). P. 12.
19	100	Guitierrez, Gustavo, *Two Theological Perspectives, Liberation Theology and Progressivist Theology,* (Maryknoll, 1978), p. 243.
20	101	Magee, Bryan, *"The Manchester Guardian Weekly,"* January 24, 1982.
21	101	Guitierrez, p. 247
22	101	Ibid.
23	107	Rada.
24	123	Crossan, John Dominic, *The Dark Interval,* (Argus, 1975).

Beard, Charles and Mary R., *Basic History of the United States,*
    New Home Library, N.Y., 1944

Berger, Peter, *Lectures on religion and Modern Consciousness*
    at the Vancouver School of Theology, July 1975

Berton, Pierre (ed.), *Canada's Illustrated Heritage Series,*
    Natural Science of Canada Ltd., Toronto, 1978

Bibby, Reginald W., *Canadian Commitment,* United Church of Canada,
    Toronto, September 1979

Bibby, Reginald W., *Religion and Modernity: The Canadian Case,*
    Journal for the Scientific Study of Religion, June 1979

Bibby, Reginald W., *The State of Collective Religiosity in Canada,*
    The Canadian Review of Sociology and Anthropology, February 1979

Broadfoot, Barry, *The Pioneer Years, 1895-1914—Memoirs of Settlers*
    Who Opened the West, Doubleday Canada Ltd., 1976

Canada and Latin America in the 1980s—Alternatives for Development,
    Inter-Church Committee on Human Rights in Latin America, April 1981

Crockett, W.R., *Political Theology in British Columbia,* in *The Ecumenist,*
    Vol 20, no 1, Nov-Dec 1981 pps 11-16 Paulist Press, Toronto

Crossan, John Dominic, *The Dark Interval,* Argus Communications, 1975

Crossan, John Dominic, *In Parables,* Harper and Row, 1973

Crysdale, Stewart, *The Changing Church in Canada,*
    United Church of Canada, 1965

Green, Michael, *Evangelism in the Early Church,*
    London, Hodder & Stoughton, 1970

Guitierrez, Gustavo, *Two Theological Perspectives, Liberation Theology*
    and Progressivist Theology, Maryknoll, 1978

Kebler, Werner H., *The Kingdom in Mark,* Fortress Press, 1974

Kilbourn, William, *Religion in Canada—The Spiritual Development*
    of a Nation, McLelland and Stewart, 1968

Knight, James (ed.) *Canada, the Formative Years,* Imperial Oil Review, 1967

Lefever, Ernest, *Amsterdam to Nairobi,* Ethics & Policy Center, Wash. 1979

Lekachman, Robert, *A History of Economic Ideas,* McGraw-Hill, 1976

Magee, Bryan, *The Manchester Guardian Weekly,* January 24, 1982

Maxwell, Grant, *Signs and Portents of the Seventies—Attitudes*
    at the Canadian Gransroots, Canadian Catholic Conference, Nov. 1975

Oliver, Dennis, *The New Canadian Religious Plurality,* 1979

Perrin, Norman, *The Kingdom of God in the Teaching of Jesus,*
    London, S.C.M., 1963

Potter, Phillip, *What in the World is the World Council of Churches?*
    Risk Book Series, World Council of Churches, Geneva, 1978

Profile Studies—Canada's Religious Composition, Statistics Canada, 1976

Rada, Juan F., *The Microelectronics Revolution; Implications for the*
    Third World, in *Development Dialogue* 2/1982 pps 41-67

Roddan, Sam, *Batter My Heart,* United Church of Canada, Vancouver 1975

Toffler, Alvin, *The Third Wave,* Wm. Morrow, N.Y., 1980

van den Heuvel, Albert, *Shalom and Combat,* Risk Book Series,
    World Council of Churches, Geneva, 1979

Walsh, H.H., *The Christian Church in Canada,* Ryerson, Toronto, 1956

Wilson, Douglas J., *The Church Grows in Canada,* Canadian Council
    of Churches, 1966

Your Kingdom Come—Report on the World Conference on Mission and
    Evangelism, Melbourne, 1980, World Council of Churches, Geneva, 1980